Historic Sites of Texas

By

June Rayfield Welch

Library of Congress Catalog Card No.
72-904-35

First Printing Nov. 1972

Published by
G.L.A. Press
Dallas, Texas

Printed
by

Waco, Texas

Dedication

To my grandparents,

Owen Rayfield Welch, born August 24, 1883, in Wise County, died August 10, 1946, in Bell County,

Susan Joanna King, born March 12, 1884, in Cleburne County, Alabama,

James Marion Prigmore, born November 9, 1875, in Collin County, died March 19, 1972, in Tarrant County,

Ellen Frances Owens, born October 14, 1877, in Wise County,

who saw Texas grow into a great state.

Introduction

When I was a peaceful little kid in Gainesville there were several weeds in my garden. Among them were contentious big kids, Sunday school, liver and onions, chiggers, and socks that would never stay up. And there was Texas history: it was deadly dull.

Of course, the main problem was me. But there were contributing factors. For instance, the textbook never mentioned anything about Cooke County, although I knew Gainesville had a history, that California Street took its name from the forty-niners who passed that way hoping for a share of Sutter's Fort gold.

According to the book — which I had carefully wrapped, on the first day of school, in a brown paper cover with Crystal Creamery advertising — everything of historic importance had occurred somewhere else. This, plus the drowsiness induced by a warm Texas afternoon and a recent lunch of a nickel hamburger, a Woosie's Root Beer, and a moon pie gave an unreal, other-worldly quality to the state's past. Except for the long story of governors succeeding one another, it seemed that Texas history was an assortment of events at places that had never been, or had ceased to exist.

Texas history did not believe in Gainesville, and I did not believe in it. The sole exception was the Alamo. I knew it existed because a relative visiting a faith-healer on the Rio Grande had sent a postcard with a photograph of some rumble-seated Model A's parked in front of the old mission.

In time I outgrew those curious attitudes. I went to college, wrote a thesis, and taught courses in Texas history. Then, in 1969, Larry Nance and I set out to photograph the state's 254 courthouses, taking the counties in tiers and working clock-wise from northeast Texas. And when we reached Goliad I was surprised and pleased and sorry that I had not believed and attended to what had been taught so long ago.

I wanted then to see all the great places of Texas' past, to photograph the sites as they are now for those who sit in quiet classrooms and study Texas history.

I wanted also to write about those happenings and people left out of, or barely noticed in, the textbooks. By using a site format it would be possible to treat subjects that usually fall down between the cracks, but which, when caught, make history live.

Not long after I started photographing sites it was apparent that there were too many interesting places and stories for one book. Since another would be required, I did not try for a balance in time or locale in this volume. This collection of seventy-two sites emphasizes the early periods and old Texas. The volume now in progress moves south and west of San Antonio and well into this century.

Barbara Larrabee of the Institute of Texan Cultures was especially helpful in assembling the old photographs; Larry Nance designed the dust jacket; and Clara Stahl, of Waco, typed the manuscript until she knew it by heart.

June Rayfield Welch
Dallas
September, 1972

Table of Contents and Sites

1   Glen Rose Was Dinosaur Country (Somervell County)   2
2   Mound Builders Lived in East Texas (Cherokee County)   8
3   The Karankawa Were Cannibals (Galveston County) 10
4   Cabeza de Vaca Was Wrecked on the Texas Coast (Galveston County) 12
5   La Salle Built a Fort in Victoria County (Victoria County) 16
6   La Salle Was Killed Near Navasota (Grimes County) 18
7   Missionaries Would Hold Texas for Spain (Houston County) 22
8   A City Would Grow Up at San Pedro Springs (Bexar County) 24
9   Mission Guadalupe Was to Serve the Nacogdoche (Nacogdoches County) 26
10 Father Olivares Founded San Antonio (Bexar County) 28
11 San José Was the Queen of the Missions (Bexar County) 30
12 Canary Islanders Came to San Antonio (Bexar County) 36
13 Concepción Is the Oldest Unrestored Church (Bexar County) 38
14 San Francisco Mission Was Moved to San Antonio (Bexar County) 42
15 San Juan Honors the Warrior Saint (Bexar County) 44
16 Espada Has a 230-Year Old Aqueduct (Bexar County) 46
17 The Goliad Mission Was Moved from Lavaca Bay (Goliad County) 48
18 Gil Ybarbo Settled Nacogdoches Without Consent (Nacogdoches County) 50
19 Ybarbo Built the Stone Fort (Nacogdoches County) 52
20 Philip Nolan Traded in Mustangs (Hill County) 54
21 Aury Was a Privateer (Galveston County) 56
22 Lafitte Operated from Galveston (Galveston County) 58
23 Jane Long Ran a Richmond Hotel (Fort Bend County) 62
24 Moses Austin Traveled the Camino Real (Bexar County) 66
25 Stephen Austin Carried Out His Father's Plan (Austin County) 68
26 Jared Groce Brought Ninety Slaves with Him (Waller County) 70
27 Austin's Town Was at a Good Brazos Crossing (Austin County) 72
28 A Mexican Fort Was Captured at Velasco (Brazoria County) 76
29 Daniel Parker Founded Pilgrim Church (Anderson County) 78
30 Vice President Anderson Died at the Fanthorp Inn (Grimes County) 82
31 Robertson Founded Nashville-on-the-Brazos (Milam County) 84
32 Santa Anna Overwhelmed the Alamo (Bexar County) 86
33 Fannin Surrendered at the Coleto (Goliad County) 88
34 Santa Anna Ordered the Goliad Prisoners' Execution (Goliad County) 90
35 The Goliad Prisoners Were Buried in a Common Grave (Goliad County) 94
36 Dilue Harris Was in the Runaway Scrape (Colorado County) 96

37 The Armies Camped Opposite Each Other at Columbus (Colorado County) 98

38 Deaf Smith Was the Texas Spy (Fort Bend County) 100

39 Houston Took It All at San Jacinto (Harris County) 102

40 Noah T. Byars Brought the Convention to Washington (Washington County) . . .104

41 The Texans Declared Their Independence (Washington County) 106

42 Treaties of Peace Were Signed at Velasco (Brazoria County) 108

43 The Comanche Swept Down on Fort Parker (Limestone County) 110

44 The First Masonic Lodge Met Under an Oak Tree (Brazoria County) 114

45 Houston Was the Second Capital (Harris County) 116

46 Three-Legged Willie Carried the Constitution on His Hip (Colorado County) . . .118

47 Rangers Camped on the Site of Waco (McLennan County) 122

48 Walter Lane Escaped the Battle Creek Fight (Navarro County) 124

49 Lamar Believed Texas Would Extend to the Pacific (Fort Bend County) 126

50 At the Neches the Cherokee Were Expelled (Van Zandt County) 128

51 Bullock's Pigs Disrupted Diplomatic Relations (Travis County) 132

52 Houston Was Baptized at Independence Church (Washington County) 134

53 John Neely Bryan Founded Dallas (Dallas County) 136

54 Anson Jones Was the Republic's Last President (Washington County) 138

55 French Utopians Settled La Reunion (Dallas County) 140

56 The Mier Prisoners Were Buried at La Grange (Fayette County) 142

57 Houston's Defense Counsel Was Francis Scott Key (Walker County) 144

58 Sam Houston Believed in the Union (Walker County) 146

59 General Twiggs Surrendered at the Main Plaza (Bexar County) 150

60 Forty-Two Men Died in Gainesville's Great Hangings (Cooke County) 152

61 The Chisholm Trail Was a Beef Highway (Hill County) 154

62 Sam Bass Intended to Rob a Round Rock Bank (Williamson County) 158

63 Captain King Died at the Menger Hotel (Bexar County) 160

64 Ike Thought He Was Born in Tyler (Grayson County) .162

65 O. Henry Was an Austin Bank Teller (Travis County) .166

66 Lieutenant Foulois Was the American Air Force (Bexar County) 168

67 The Battleship Texas Was at Iwo Jima (Harris County) 170

68 The Grandcamp Exploded at Texas City (Galveston County) 172

69 John Kennedy Was Slain at the Triple Underpass (Dallas County) 174

70 Oswald Was Captured in the Texas Theater (Dallas County) 176

71 A Presidential Library Was Built in Austin (Travis County) 178

72 Glen Rose Got Sinclair's Dinosaurs (Somervell County) 182

Historic Sites of Texas

Glen Rose Was Dinosaur Country

Early Glen Rose residents wondered about the large three-toed fossil footprints in the flat limestone along the Paluxy River. They remained unknown to science until geologist Ellis W. Shuler classified them in 1917.

In 1938, Ernest T. Adams, of Somervell County, confirmed the presence of another type of fossil footprint. Adams, an honor graduate of Baylor University and a Rhodes Scholar, took two degrees from Oxford University. He was a municipal bond lawyer in Dallas until he returned to Glen Rose in 1936. There he practiced law as little as possible — for years he was the only attorney in the county — and devoted fourteen hour days to exploring Somervell's past.

Adams was among the first to quarry the huge, birdlike, three-toed tracks, one of which is still in the bandstand wall on the courthouse square. Like Shuler, Adams recognized them as tracks of biped carnivorous dinosaurs, powerful predators that — 120 million years before — preyed on other dinosaurs ranging the shores of a long, low, coastal area roughly parallelling the present Gulf of Mexico. But Adams was caught up in the study of ancient man. The dinosaur tracks remained only a local curiosity.

In 1938, Roland T. Bird, of the Department of Vertebrate Paleontology at New York's Museum of Natural History, while winding up a New Mexico field trip learned of Glen Rose as a site to prospect for dinosaur trails.

Bird was an associate of Dr. Barnum Brown, the Museum's famed authority on dinosaurs. For many years, as Brown's trusted assistant, Bird had studied dinosaur trails. In 1937 he had obtained for Brown from a Colorado coal mine an 18,000 pound slab containing two gigantic iguanodon footprints. Except for the Texas Cretaceous, Bird had prospected or collected from nearly all the numerous track localities in the United States.

At Glen Rose, Bird learned that Adams was out of town, but that Jim Ryals, a farmer, had also quarried some carnosaur footprints. Ryals showed Bird a fine trail consisting of several right and left prints; it had been made by an early ancestral cousin of *Tyrannosaurus rex*, one of Barnum Brown's spectacular discoveries. The tracks averaged twenty-six inches in length. This dinosaur measured thirty-three feet from nose to tail tip, stood thirteen feet tall, and had a seven foot stride.

Ryals spoke of having seen huge round footprints that had since been destroyed by erosion. Bird wondered if Ryals had come upon a sauropod trail, a type then unknown to science. The sauropod dinosaur — often termed brontosaur after the best known genus — was the most gigantic of all dinosaurs. They were herbivorous quadrupeds. All had variations of long necks and tails; all inhabited shoreline environments where a suitable depth of water would help support bodies ranging in weight from twenty to eighty tons.

At first opportunity Bird sought out Ernest Adams, who confirmed Ryals' story. Adams' suggestion as to where to look next only led to another site where heavy erosion had been at work.

The preservation of such tracks in prehistoric times depended on thick plastic mud that would retain good prints even under water. Days or weeks later, gentle currents, silt-laden, buried the tracks with fresh mud. In time, succeeding deposits had been swept

Hundreds of dinosaur tracks, made millions of years ago, are to be found along the Paluxy River in Somervell County. These are west of Glen Rose.

in by a sea that eventually covered most of Texas. Millions of years later — the sea having drained away — erosion by rivers and streams cut into the strata, now hardened to stone, and gradually uncovered the old track-bearing horizons, sometimes destroying the prints in the process.

While prospecting downstream from Ryals' farm Bird encountered, in the local trackway horizon, a huge mud-filled depression, the print of a brontosaur's right hind foot. Exploring farther, Bird waded into several complete trails under mud on the river bottom.

Here were no simple carnosaur trails, no narrow lines of right and left prints, but six-foot wide trackways of the four-footed brontosaurs. The forefeet were nearly round and clawless; the hind feet were often thirty-eight inches long by twenty wide, with four stumpy claws on the broad front end. No signs of dragging tails were found; the water had been deep enough to float them.

At the American Museum, Barnum Brown conceived the idea of displaying a thirty-foot section of trackway on the base with the mounted brontosaur skeleton. Placed behind the back feet, under the long tail, the illusion could be created of the great sixty-seven foot "Thunder Lizard" in motion, leaving a trail. In 1940, through the assistance of the Works Progress Administration, Bird returned to Glen Rose. The Sinclair Oil Company also contributed funds. Labor was recruited locally.

Selecting a trail from which a long, uneroded portion could be uncovered by removing undisturbed overburden at the river's edge, Bird began the five month project. Hundreds of spectators from all over Texas came to watch.

The trail lay in a twenty-six inch layer of rock. It was broken into blocks, which were wrapped and numbered for re-assembly. The fifteen ton slab going to the American Museum was in 118 blocks. A shorter section went to the University of Texas at Austin. Ernest Adams took a four track section for Baylor University, and other blocks, with from one to three tracks, were sent to Brooklyn College, Southern Methodist University, and the Smithsonian Institution. A total of forty tons of material was removed from the Paluxy.

While uncovering the trail, Bird and his workers were surprised to find that a large carnosaur apparently had charged the brontosaur. Both had been wading in shallow water not far from where the hungry carnivore must have left the nearby prehistoric shore. The charging predator had splashed repeatedly in his prospective victim's footprints. As the pursued sought to escape, the unswerving trail of the carnosaur followed on the brontosaur's heels.

After a hundred feet of this chase was uncovered, the project ran out of funds. What happened next is hidden under the remaining overburden. Both Austin and New York brontosaur trackway exhibits are complete with prints of the charging carnosaur.

4

—Roland T. Bird
To remove the brontosaur trail from the Paluxy, workmen had to cut the rock slab into blocks. These were wrapped and numbered for reassembly.

—Roland T. Bird
Part of the Paluxy River trail was taken to the American Museum of Natural History in New York City and set behind a brontosaur skeleton. The three-toed prints paralleling the great tracks were made by a carnosaur who perhaps hoped for a brontosaur lunch.

6

Jim Ryals, a depression era Glen Rose farmer, sold quarried dinosaur tracks. Iron bands prevented the rock from breaking.

7

Mound Builders Lived in East Texas

Although there are more than 100,000 man-made mounds in the United States — 500 in Ross County, Ohio alone — Texas has only a handful. All are in the northeastern part of the state.

Of the mounds in the United States, some were for burial purposes and some were platforms for wooden temples. Some bore the shape of men and some depicted animals. Ohio's Great Serpent Mound is 1,330 feet long. The Poverty Point, Louisiana mounds contained 550,000 cubic yards of earth. The largest mound required three million man hours of labor, 822 men working ten-hour days for a year.

Mound Street in Nacogdoches lay between four small artificial hills. All but one were leveled so that houses might be built. The survivor is at 516 Mound Street.

One of the largest of the Texas mounds is twelve miles northwest of Texarkana. Another, about the same size, is at Mound Prairie, Cherokee County, six miles southwest of Alto. Both were temple mounds, built with innumerable basket-loads of clay. They are about twelve feet high and 150 feet long.

Villages of the mound builders were near rivers. Their houses were round and made of upright poles and thatch. A central square adjoined the mound, on top of which the temple was situated. The people farmed, fished, and hunted with the bow and arrow.

The top of the hill at Mound Prairie is rectangular and flat. In its early life it accommodated a temple of wood which sheltered the perpetual fire considered sacred by the Creek and other Indians of the southeastern United States. After the mound builders died out or moved, other Indians used the high ground for homesites or camping. The hill was not subject to flooding and afforded a view of the countryside.

The Texas mounds were probably built between 1300 and 1700 A.D. The builders artificially flattened the skull, a practice found throughout the United States. Lewis and Clark reported that some Pacific Coast tribes, such as the Chinook, shaped the heads of their infants by placing them in a press for several months. The natural shape was never restored, so that there was a straight line from the tip of the nose to the top of the skull, with a thickness of only a couple of inches above the forehead.

At Mound Prairie, six miles southwest of Alto, Cherokee County, on State Highway 21, is one of the largest Indian mounds in Texas.

The Karankawa Were Cannibals

The Karankawa tribes lived along the coast from Galveston to Corpus Christi. Although they barely extracted a living from the coastal plain, they were large, handsome people.

The Indians Cabeza de Vaca met when he was cast ashore on Malhado Isle in 1528 were probably Karankawa. A century and a half thereafter the Karankawa cooperated with the elements in destroying La Salle's colony. The Spanish founded the mission Nuestra Señora del Refugio to minister to them in 1791, with little luck. The Kronks — a name supplied by the Austin colonists — were a nuisance out of proportion to their numbers. They had died out or moved to Mexico by the time Texas became independent.

The men wore no clothes and pierced their breasts and lower lips to hold decorative lengths of cane. In 1768, Father Gasper José de Solís wrote that the women dressed decently and that, "They paint themselves in stripes all over, different figures being formed with the stripes, now of animals, now of birds, now of flowers." Of the Karankawa generally he said, "All of the Indian men and women are bad tempered and ungrateful except now and then one who is affectionate."

The Karankawa were nomads. They fished and took oysters and clams in season and then journeyed inland to hunt and pick berries and nuts. When other food was scarce they turned to lice and locusts, and practiced cannibalism. They spent only a few weeks at a campsite but returned there from year to year.

Often Karankawa dwellings had one wall, offering shelter only from the windward side. A warrior used a bow as tall as he was — and the Karankawa were six footers — and of extraordinary power.

Cabeza de Vaca wrote of Karankawa generosity to one another, "They have a custom when they meet, or from time to time when they visit, of remaining half an hour before they speak, weeping; and this over, he that is visited first rises and gives the other all he has, which is received, and after a little while he carries it away, and often goes without saying a word."

Their kindliness did not extend to Cabeza de Vaca, who "resolved to flee from them . . . the life I led being insupportable. Besides much other labor, I had to get out roots from below the water, and from among the cane where they grew in the ground. From this employment I had my fingers so worn that did a straw but touch them they would bleed."

Three centuries later an early storekeeper named Buckner hoped for an early Kronk extinction. When some Tonkawa sought ammunition to wipe out the Karankawa, Buckner was pleased. When the Karankawa begged ammunition to use against the Tonkawa, he was elated; Tonks were worse than Kronks. Buckner was happy to assist a mutual genocide.

On the day of battle Buckner watched through a field glass as Kronks poured onto a prairie, firing and yelling. From a stand of trees half a mile away came the Tonks answering in kind. Both sides were out of rifle range. While Buckner urged them to get close, all the ammunition was used up. Not a soul was hit, but each side claimed a great victory.

The Karankawa roamed the coastal plain and lived at the level of the Stone Age. One of their Galveston Island campsites was excavated at Jamaica Beach in the late sixties.

Cabeza de Vaca Was Wrecked on the Texas Coast

On the morning of November 6, 1528, Alvar Núñez Cabeza de Vaca and about eighty other Spaniards were cast ashore on a long, narrow island on the Texas coast. The Spaniards were survivors of the Pánfilo de Narváez expedition. Only fifteen would remain alive when spring came. They called the place Malhado, the Isle of Misfortune.

Malhado was probably Galveston Island, if Cabeza de Vaca incorrectly estimated its size. Otherwise, Velasco Island most nearly fits his description, although it is a peninsula, not an island.

But the identity of Malhado Island is of secondary consequence. The real significance of the Spaniards' being stranded on the Gulf coast was that it precipitated the first exploration of the Texas interior by Europeans. Cabeza de Vaca's narrative of his seven and one-half years in the empty vastness of the Southwest is one of the world's great adventure stories.

Born in the province of Cadiz, Spain, Alvar Núñez Cabeza de Vaca was the son of Francisco de Vera. He took the name of his mother, Teresa Cabeza de Vaca. Her ancestor, a shepherd, had been given his name by the King of Navarre. In July, 1212, the shepherd, whose name had been Martín Alhaja, had guided the king's army through a pass, using the skull of a cow to mark the way. The army won a major victory and Alhaja became Martín Cabeza de Vaca, Martín "Cow's Head."

Alvar Núñez Cabeza de Vaca came to the new world as treasurer of the Narváez expedition in 1527. A commission to colonize territory north of Mexico had been granted Narváez. The expedition landed on Florida's west coast in April, 1528.

Narváez, with 300 men, intended to go overland and meet his ships on the west coast of the Gulf of Mexico. His party disappeared into the jungle. After a year of searching for Narváez the ships proceeded to Mexico.

Meanwhile Narváez was using up his men and supplies looking for rich cities. When it was obvious that they would perish otherwise, Narváez had boats built. The Spaniards ate their horses and used the hides for water bottles. They made sails of their shirts and put to sea in five crude boats; the most seaworthy were wrecked on Malhado. Narváez was never heard of again.

Cabeza de Vaca and the other survivors were captured by primitive coastal Indians. After years of servitude Cabeza de Vaca and three other Spaniards escaped. They journeyed into the interior to avoid recapture. Cabeza de Vaca's companions were Andrés Dorantes de Carranza, Alonzo del Castillo Maldonado, and Estevanico, of Azamor, Morocco, the black slave of Dorantes.

Although none of the Spaniards had any medical training, they moved among the tribes as physicians. At first their medical skills consisted of praying over their patients. But the Indians treated the Spaniards as mighty healers and, in time, they developed confidence in their own abilities.

Cabeza de Vaca performed what was probably the first surgery in Texas. He said, "They fetched a man to me and stated that a long time since he had been wounded by an arrow in the right shoulder, and that the point of the shaft was lodged above his heart,

Cabeza de Vaca, of the Narváez expedition, landed near present Tampa, Florida, wandered westward, put to sea in primitive boats, and was washed ashore on the Texas coast.

which, he said, gave him much pain, and, in consequence, he was always sick. Probing the wound I felt the arrow-head, and found it had passed through the cartilage. With a knife I carried, I opened the breast to the place, and saw the point was aslant and troublesome to take out.

"I continued to cut, and putting in the point of the knife, at last with great difficulty I drew the head forth. It was very large.

"With the bone of a deer, and by virtue of my calling," (note the professional attitude) "I made two stitches that threw the blood over me, and with a hair from a skin I stanched the flow .... The next day I cut the two stitches and the Indian was well. The wound I made appeared only like a seam in the palm of the hand."

Cabeza de Vaca had been without clothing since attempting to refloat his boat on the morning after it capsized at Malhado. So weak were the Spaniards that clothes were a burden. They stripped and put everything in the boat. Then a great wave took away the boat and all their possessions. Later he wrote, "I have already stated that throughout all this country we went naked, and as we were accustomed to being so, twice a year we cast our skins like serpents."

The Spaniards continued westward. In the spring of 1536 they encountered Spanish slave traders in upper Sonora and were taken to Culiacán. Eight years after landing near Tampa Bay in Florida, Cabeza de Vaca and his three companions reached civilization. Cabeza de Vaca wrote, "Arrived at Compostela, the Governor entertained us graciously and gave us of his clothing for our use. I could not wear any for some time, nor could we sleep anywhere but on the ground."

On July 26, 1536, the Spaniards reached Mexico City. Although they had seen no wealthy countries, their reports stimulated the Spanish belief that rich cities lay to the north. One result was the expedition of Francisco Vásquez de Coronado to find the Seven Cities of Cibola.

Cabeza de Vaca was made governor of the provinces of Rio de la Plata, but his tenure in Paraguay was stormy. He was arrested in 1543 and sent back to Spain. After eight years he was finally tried and banished to Africa. Later the conviction was reversed, and he died at Seville in 1555 or 1557.

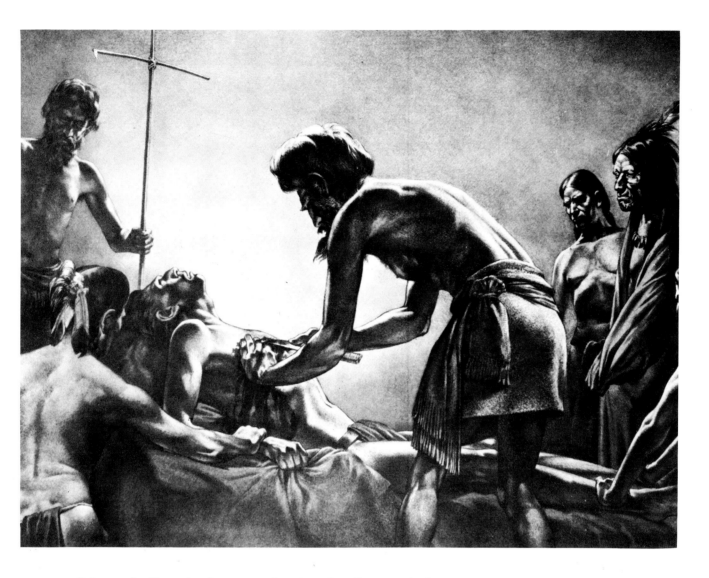

Cabeza de Vaca is shown performing the first surgical operation on Texas soil by a European in this painting by famed artist Tom Lea, from Sparkman's *The Texas Surgical Society, The First Fifty Years.*

La Salle Built a Fort in Victoria County

For almost two centuries after the Spaniards arrived in the new world the Texas interior remained unsettled. When finally a colony was founded it was French, but it provoked Spain to the efforts which would result in the Spanish settlement of Texas.

René Robert Cavelier, Sieur de la Salle, was born at Rouen, France, November 22, 1643. Just prior to ordination as a Jesuit priest, La Salle left the order. He followed his brother to Canada in 1666. From Indians who came to his trading post near Montreal La Salle learned of the great Ohio River. For a dozen years he explored the interior of the continent.

In mid-winter, 1682, La Salle started down the Mississippi River. He reached the Gulf of Mexico on April 8. At the mouth of the Mississippi he erected a cross and, in behalf of France, took possession of all territory drained by the river. He called it Louisiana for Louis XIV.

After being commissioned to establish a colony in Louisiana, La Salle sailed from France in August, 1684. By mistake he landed on the Texas coast in January, 1685.

La Salle left Henri Joutel in charge of the temporary fort while he and some fifty men located a permanent site, planted corn, and tried to determine whether Matagorda Bay was an outlet of the Mississippi River. Of the 120 colonists left behind, Joutel said, "Some of them died every day of scurvy, homesickness and other ills."

At the permanent site, a few miles inland on Garcitas Creek, Fort St. Louis was built. Drought and animals destroyed the crops. The colonists died of disease and starvation. La Salle was killed while seeking help for the settlement.

In the meantime the Spaniards, determined to keep out foreigners, sent expeditions to find the French. When Captain Alonso de León discovered Fort St. Louis, in 1689, it was abandoned. Father Damian Massanet said, "We arrived about eleven in the forenoon, and found six small houses, built with poles, plastered with mud, and roofed over with buffalo hides. There was another large house where pigs were kept; and a wooden fort made from the hulk of a wrecked vessel . . . There was a great lot of shattered weapons, broken by the Indians — firelocks, carbines, cutlasses . . . . We found two unburied bodies, which I interred, setting up a cross over the grave. There were also many torn up books and a number of dead pigs."

In 1914, using Spanish maps made in 1690, Dr. Herbert Eugene Bolton located Fort St. Louis on the Claude Keeran ranch near Placedo, Victoria County. He wrote, "From the surface of the ground I gathered a handful of small fragments of antique blue and white porcelain . . . . Mr. Keeran told . . . of the unearthing on the spot, some thirty years ago, of half of an immense copper kettle, nearly a yard in diameter." The kettle and other artifacts were probably from the Spanish presidio built on the French ruins in 1722.

The site of Fort St. Louis near Placedo, Victoria County, is covered by dense brush although it was cleared and excavated to a depth of one foot less than five years ago

La Salle Was Killed Near Navasota

From the beginning La Salle's settlement was in jeopardy. The Fort St. Louis site was not a good one. The nearest timber was more than two miles away. Since there were no horses or wagons to haul the wood needed for buildings, the men had to drag the logs over rough terrain to the site. Already weakened, they became ill from the hard work. Many died.

Some of the hardships were unavoidable, but some resulted from La Salle's stubbornness. To minimize labor Joutel suggested that timbers already felled and left at the first camp be floated upstream. Joutel said, ". . . but as he had said a number of times before, he wanted no advice."

Father Massanet wrote in 1689, "This place affords no advantages of situation, for good drinking water is very far off, and timber still further. The water of the stream is very brackish, so much so that in five days during which the camp was pitched here, all the horses sickened. The Indians dig wells for drinking water."

La Salle's first journey to bring supplies to the failing colony was cut short by his illness. In January, 1687, a last desperate attempt was made to locate the Mississippi and follow it north to French settlements. La Salle took seventeen men with him. Twenty remained at Fort St. Louis.

On March 1 La Salle sent Duhaut, Hiens, Liotot, Saget, and an Indian guide for corn and beans he had cached nearby. The supplies had been ruined, but Duhaut's men killed two buffalo. Duhaut notified La Salle that they were curing the buffalo meat; La Salle sent Moranger to bring some of it to his men.

There was already bad blood between Moranger and the others. After a quarrel over the buffalo meat, Duhaut's party decided to kill Moranger, Saget, and the Indian.

Joutel wrote, "They waited until night, when the unfortunate wretches had eaten supper and were asleep. Then Liotot, the inhuman executioner, took an ax and began with Moranger. He crushed his head with many blows of the ax, and then did the same with the servant (Saget) and the Indian, while his fellow villains stood on guard ready to shoot if any of them resisted."

The murderers knew La Salle would have to be killed to save them from punishment. When Moranger did not return, La Salle went after him. La Salle, approaching Duhaut's camp somewhere in the vicinity of present Navasota, shot at some buzzards. The murderers hid and waited for him.

Joutel, who was a few miles away, said that La Salle had not bothered to reload his gun after firing at the birds, that Duhaut shot him through the head, and then, "he dropped dead on the spot, without speaking a word."

Henri de Tonti, who had remained at Fort St. Louis, believed Duhaut and Liotot had always wanted to kill La Salle. He said the conspirators hid after hearing La Salle's shot and, "As M. de la Salle advanced . . . He received three balls in the head, and fell down dead . . . ."

The murderers, afraid to return to a French settlement, were enslaved by Indians who later turned them over to the Spaniards.

René Robert Cavelier, Sieur de La Salle, claimed for France all territory drained by the Mississippi and named it Louisiana for Louis XIV.

John Keeran was a small boy when Professor Bolton located the site of Fort St. Louis on his father's ranch.

RENÉ ROBERT CAVELIER
SIEUR DE LA SALLE

TREACHEROUSLY SLAIN BY HIS OWN
MEN NEAR THIS SPOT IN MARCH 1687

BORN ROUEN, FRANCE, NOVEMBER 22, 1643
EXPLORER OF THE MISSISSIPPI RIVER
FRONTIER STATESMAN-EMPIRE BUILDER
A NOBLEMAN IN RANK AND CHARACTER

ERECTED BY
THE TEXAS SOCIETY
OF THE DAUGHTERS OF THE
AMERICAN REVOLUTION AND
THE CITIZENS OF NAVASOTA
1930

La Salle was on his way to get help for his failing colony when one of his men shot him near present Navasota, Grimes County.

Missionaries Would Hold Texas For Spain

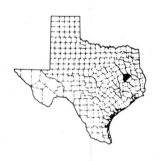

Because of their fears of French intrusion, the Spaniards established the first mission in Texas, San Francisco de los Tejas. The Spaniards had no immediate interest in Texas. They were fully occupied in the development of Mexico and Peru. But they did not want the big, empty land to fall into French hands. Until such time as settlement became desirable, Texas was a valuable buffer protecting Mexico from foreigners.

La Salle's landing worried the Spanish viceroy long after the demise of Fort St. Louis. In March, 1690, he sent Captain Alonso de León and Father Massanet to destroy the ruins of Fort St. Louis. No evidence was to remain to support a French claim. Father Massanet said, "I myself set fire to the fort, and as there was a high wind — the wood, by the way, was from the Frenchman's sloop, which had sunk on entering the bay — in half an hour the fort was in ashes."

The other task assigned De León and Massanet was to establish a mission among the Caddo confederacies of East Texas. The Caddo tribes were the most stable of the Texas Indians. They were agriculturalists and were located near the French settlements. Since Spain was short of money and people, it would be difficult to place either an army or colonists in Texas. But if a few missionaries could make Christians and Spaniards of the East Texas Indians, they would constitute a vigorous new population blocking any French advance.

Father Massanet found an appropriate site for the mission of San Francisco in a Tejas village near present Weches, "a delightful spot close to the brook, with fine woods, and plum trees like those in Spain. Soon afterwards, on the same day, they began to fell trees and cart the wood, and within three days we had a roomy dwelling and a church wherein to say mass."

On June 1, 1690, the church was consecrated. The soldiers were given permission to fire their rifles during the procession and at the close of the mass. On the following day Father Massanet departed for Mexico, leaving behind three priests and three soldiers. Father Massanet said, "Captain de León left for the soldiers nine of the king's horses, some firelocks, a barrel of powder and some shot; and for the priests he left twenty-six loads of flour, twenty cows, two yoke of oxen, ploughs with ploughshares, axes, spades and other little things."

The mission was abandoned in 1693 after the Indians became hostile. Before they fled, the priests burned the church. In 1716, when it appeared that the French were about to move into Texas, the mission was re-established and five other missions were founded. A minor French invasion three years later caused all of the East Texas missions to be abandoned.

In 1721 the Marquis de Aguayo reopened the mission, as San Francisco de los Neches, a few miles from the original site. Finally the mission was moved to San Antonio and became San Francisco de la Espada.

The Franciscans placed their first mission in forested East Texas near the present town of Weches, Houston County, where this replica is located.

A City Would Grow Up at San Pedro Springs

After establishing the San Francisco mission Father Damian Massanet returned to Mexico City urging the expansion of missionary activity. The viceroy was receptive.

Don Domingo Terán de los Rios, governor of Coahuila and Texas, was ordered to supply the San Francisco mission, to see if any Frenchmen were in Texas, and to consider the feasibility of founding additional missions. The East Texas Indians, Christianized and loyal to the crown, would constitute a barrier the French could not pass.

Terán, with fifty soldiers and fourteen Franciscans, reached — on June 13, 1691, the feast day of Saint Anthony — a river which he named San Antonio de Padua. The next day the company remained at the river to celebrate the feast of Corpus Christi. A company of Payaya Indians lived there and named the place Yanaguana. Terán called the country the most beautiful in New Spain and thought it a splendid mission site.

In East Texas Terán found that the San Francisco mission had not done well and decided, from this and other evidence, that a missionary effort could not succeed in Texas. In 1693 the mission San Francisco was abandoned; the Indians were preparing to drive out the missionaries.

In 1709, Captain Pedro de Aguirre and fourteen soldiers accompanied Father Antonio de San Buenaventura Olivares and Father Isidro Felix de Espinosa to the site of San Antonio. On April 13 they discovered and named San Pedro Springs, whose water was sufficient for a town, Father Espinosa said.

Spanish interest in Texas waned until another French scare provoked the Domingo Ramón expedition in 1716. From that time on there would always be at least one Spanish settlement in the Texas interior. On May 14 the Spaniards reached San Pedro Springs.

The missions founded by Ramón made expedient the establishment of a settlement between East Texas and the Rio Grande, which complemented Father Olivares' desire to locate a mission on the San Antonio River.

In April, 1718, the expedition of Governor Martín de Alarcón crossed the Rio Grande. There were seventy-two persons in the party. On the first of May Alarcón founded the mission San Antonio de Valero near San Pedro Springs. Four days later the Presidio San Antonio de Bexar was established. There is conflicting evidence concerning their precise sites, but both were located with reference to water. The chaplain wrote, "In this place of San Antonio there is a spring of water which is about three-fourths of a league from the principal river. In this locality, in the very spot on which the Villa of Bexar was founded, it is easy to secure (irrigation) water, but nowhere else."

The mission San José y San Miguel de Aguayo was located on the river in 1720, and the Canary Islanders arrived to found Villa San Fernando in March, 1731. Each of the transplanted East Texas missions was established along the San Antonio River.

Every Spanish expedition was impressed by the clear, cold water that flowed from springs in what is now San Antonio's San Pedro Park.

Mission Guadalupe Was to Serve the Nacogdoche

The Nacogdoche tribe was of the Caddoan Hasinai confederacy. In 1700 the main Nacogdoche village — which may have been called Nevantin — was located at the site of modern Nacogdoches.

When the Frenchman Louis de St. Denis journeyed clear across Texas without being challenged, the Spanish were put on notice of the vulnerability of the province. A new effort was made to make loyal Spaniards of the Caddo.

The first mission, San Francisco de los Tejas, was re-established. New missions were founded, including Nuestra Señora de Guadalupe, which was located at the principal town of the Nacogdoche by Domingo Ramón on July 9, 1716. The president of the Zacatecan College of Franciscan missionaries, Father Antonio Margil de Jesús, was given charge of the mission.

After a minor French invasion in 1719, all of the East Texas missions were abandoned. When, two years later, the Marquis de Aguayo and Father Margil returned to open the Guadalupe mission, nothing remained of the original church building.

A new church was dedicated August 18, 1721. Some 400 Indians pledged to settle at the mission after having accepted presents from the missionaries. Apparently the Indians failed to keep their promises.

Although the East Texas missions of the Querétarian College were relocated at San Antonio in 1731, the Mission Guadalupe, whose priests were of the Zacatecan College, remained at Nacogdoches. The mission did not prosper; the Nacogdoche moved their village away prior to 1752.

The Marquis de Rubí reported that not a single Indian was at the mission in 1767. In the following year the mission records showed only twelve baptisms, eight burials, and five marriages. In addition to an adobe church, there were several wooden buildings at the mission. The mission was abandoned in 1773, pursuant to Rubí's recommendation. The 1762 cession of Louisiana to Spain had, of course, eliminated the French threat.

When Antonio Gil Ybarbo founded modern Nacogdoches in 1779, his followers used the old mission buildings.

A busy Nacogdoches street adjoins the site of Mission Guadalupe.

Father Olivares Founded San Antonio

By the time the Marquis de Valero became viceroy of New Spain, Father Antonio de San Buenaventura Olivares had long been interested in locating a mission on the San Antonio River. He had founded the Mission San Francisco Solano in 1700 on the Rio Grande, where the Indian response had not been good. The Franciscan estimated that 3,000 neophytes might congregate at the San Antonio River.

The viceroy appointed Don Martín de Alarcón governor and ordered him to take possession of Texas and aid in founding Father Olivares' mission. Several months passed before Alarcón entered Texas. Father Olivares' party traveled separately. Alarcón established the Mission San Antonio de Valero on May 1, 1718, and Villa de Bexar five days later. Alarcón went on to East Texas, leaving Father Olivares in charge.

Father Olivares and three Indians he had raised from childhood built a house of brush, mud, and thatch and started getting ready to plant crops. The Indians were slow about congregating, and this was necessary if they were to be Christianized. Father Olivares blamed the absence of Indians on Alarcón's attitude. Alarcón had threatened to put them all to the sword if they would not move to the mission. That, Father Olivares reported, was "a more than sufficient reason why not an Indian stayed in this neighborhood and for leagues around. Imagine, Your Excellency, such a method of congregating Indians and settling the land!"

The first mission site is in dispute, although it was west of San Pedro Creek. One witness said it was "three quarters of a league down the creek" from San Pedro Springs. Another said it was near the springs and less than half a league along the creek. After Father Olivares broke his leg when his horse stepped through the rough bridge across San Pedro Creek, he moved the mission to the east side of the San Antonio River near where the Alamo stands.

By January, 1719, there were enough Indians to organize the mission pueblo. Alarcón appointed an Indian governor and council. In the next few months irrigation ditches were completed and crops were planted.

Mission records reflect the presence of Indians from forty different tribes between 1731 and 1745. A stone church building, begun in 1744, collapsed. A second church was under construction in 1758, but an inspector reported in 1762 that it had fallen down "because of the poor skill of the architect." Another church was attempted, but it was never finished. At secularization a dome was still lacking although mass had been said there for years. Since about 1808 it has been called the Alamo. One explanation of the name is that Mexican soldiers from a town called El Alamo were quartered there. Another story is that a grove of cottonwood trees grew nearby, and alamo means cottonwood.

In 1793, the mission was secularized and the land distributed to the Indians then resident.

The Mission San Antonio de Valero was established more than forty years before its church, which we call the Alamo, was begun.

San José Was the Queen of the Missions

In January, 1719, France declared war against Spain. When the news reached Louisiana the French captured Pensacola and planned to invade Texas.

In mid-June occurred the famous chicken defense at San Miguel de Linares, the easternmost Spanish mission, established two years earlier. M. Blondel, the commander at Natchitoches, with six French soldiers, surprised a ragged soldier, a Franciscan brother, and a flock of chickens at San Miguel. The other soldier and a priest were away on an errand.

As the Frenchmen waded into the chickens to take the two Spaniards prisoner, the chickens started to scatter; Blondel's horse, scared by the confusion, threw him. While the Frenchmen tended to Blondel, the lay brother escaped to warn other Spaniards; the Frenchmen had claimed a hundred troops were on the way. The Spanish fled. By the close of the year not a Spaniard remained between San Antonio and Louisiana.

Father Antonio Margil intended to return to East Texas when the trouble was over. In the meantime he urged establishment of a second mission on the San Antonio River. Plenty of Indians there were willing to be congregated in missions.

Father Olivares objected. The tribes Father Margil hoped to serve were enemies of the San Antonio de Valero Indians.

Overruling objections, the presidio commander chose a site three leagues from San Antonio de Valero. The neophytes to be congregated in the pueblo were given formal possession. The Indians, Castañeda wrote, "pulled grass, scattered rocks and dirt over the land, cut branches of trees, and did other things" evidencing their ownership. The commander then appointed the Indian officers of the pueblo.

Thus was begun, on February 23, 1720, the Mission San José y San Miguel de Aguayo. The early years were difficult. Raiding Apache made keeping the neophytes there difficult. In 1739, when San José was on the verge of prosperity, measles and smallpox epidemics occurred. Many of the healthy Indians fled, leaving San José with only forty-nine residents. Once the sickness was past, the Indians returned.

In 1740 the five San Antonio missions had 987 Indians. A 1749 report termed San José the most successful of the missions and said, "The mission has a priory of stone with arched corridors, and a very interesting church, capable of accommodating two thousand persons." The present church was begun in 1768, when the mission had 350 Indians. Father Juan Morfi called San José "the finest mission in this America and might well be called the queen of all others."

Secularization occurred in 1794. During a storm, in December, 1868, the church's dome and vaulted roof collapsed. Later damage was done by men using the statuary and ornamentation for target practice and by souvenir hunters who broke off pieces of the building.

Spanish priests called San Antonio's Mission San José y San Miguel de Aguayo the queen of the missions.

Rosa's window at the Mission San José has been admired for two centuries.

Part of the church exterior at the Mission San José was covered by colorful designs.

A garden grows among the ruins behind the church of the Mission San José.

The sacristy entrance is the only unrestored part of the Mission San José.

Canary Islanders Came to San Antonio

The Council of the Indies, in 1719, recommended sending Canary Islanders to Texas. Properly located they could bar French intrusions from Espíritu Santo (Matagorda Bay). Thirty-four years after La Salle's landing the Spanish king still considered that area especially vulnerable.

By 1730, when the first ten Canary Islands families arrived in Mexico, the importance of Espíritu Santo had declined; already the presidio and mission had been moved. The most suitable location for the settlers was the San Antonio River. Colonists had been sought in the Canary Islands because their soil was so unproductive that volunteers were more plentiful there than elsewhere.

The fifty-five colonists reached San Antonio on March 9, 1731. By royal order they were made hidalgos, Spanish noblemen. After their first crops were harvested the Villa de San Fernando was organized. The town was planned around the church and plaza. On July 31, the members of the first cabildo were appointed. The cabildo elected two alcaldes, the viceroy gave his approval, and Texas' first civil settlement was established. Progress was slowed by the difficulty of making a living. The cabildo offered slight leadership; not a member was literate. As hidalgos, some Canary Islanders thought they should not work.

Soon after their arrival the colonists asked that the missions assign Indian labor to them. The Franciscans objected. The Indians were lazy and hard to handle. Should colonists give them hard tasks they would run away, depleting the mission population and discouraging non-mission Indians from becoming neophytes. Futhermore the missionaries kept their Indians busy. The viceroy denied the colonists' request.

The Canary Islanders left their fields unfenced and mission livestock damaged their crops, which gave the settlers an excuse for shooting cattle whenever beef was needed. In 1745, the colonists were ordered to fence their fields and stop killing mission cattle.

By 1740 San Antonio consisted of five missions, the presidio — consisting of forty huts — and Villa San Fernando. The colonists had been too busy to build a church or public buildings. Morale was bad. The parish priest refused to perform; when asked to minister to them or let a Franciscan do so, he ordered the cabildo out of his house, locked the door, and ordered his servant to, "Bring me my guns."

Religious services were held at the presidio. The cornerstone of a parish church was laid in 1738, but after seven years the construction was almost abandoned. Every citizen was ordered to assist in the building under penalty of fines and imprisonment. A royal donation helped the church to completion about 1751.

The villa and presidio grew together to form San Fernando de Bexar, which became the capital of the province in 1773, and had a population of 1248, not counting the 550 mission residents, in 1783.

San Fernando Cathedral, damaged and repaired several times, was rebuilt in 1869, with the present church constructed around the original.

The parish church of the Canary Islanders became San Antonio's San Fernando Cathedral.

Concepción is the Oldest Unrestored Church

The dedicated Father Francisco Hidalgo precipitated the permanent settlement of Texas. After serving at San Francisco de los Tejas until its abandonment in 1693, he urged the renewal of the mission effort.

A letter Father Hidalgo wrote to French officials in Louisiana concerning the Tejas Indians was used by Governor De La Mothe Cadillac as a pretext to send Louis de St. Denis into Texas with trade goods. Louisiana's success would depend on its volume of trade, but markets in Texas and Mexico were closed by Spanish law.

The appearance of St. Denis on the Rio Grande in 1714 caused another French scare. Although the law forbade foreigners, he had crossed Texas unchallenged. The result was the Ramón expedition, ordered to strengthen Texas against French poaching. Curiously, St. Denis, who had caused the panic, was made second in command of the party. Before departing he married the granddaughter of the presidio commander who had arrested him when he arrived at San Juan Bautista two years before.

The mission San Francisco de los Tejas was re-established, with Father Hidalgo in charge, on July 5, 1716, twenty-three years after its abandonment.

A new mission, Nuestra Señora de la Purisima Concepción, was founded two days later near present Douglass, Nacogdoches County, in the chief village of the Hasinai.

After three years Concepción was abandoned because of a French invasion from Louisiana, then re-established August 6, 1721, by the Marquis de Aguayo. Presents were given four hundred Indians, and to the Hasinai chief Aguayo gave his best suit, "blue, embroidered with gold, with waistcoat of gold and silver lace."

Since Concepción did not prosper it was moved to the Colorado River near modern Austin's Zilker Park and then to the San Antonio River in 1731.

At San Antonio the mission served about thirty Coahuiltecan tribes. By 1762 Concepción's records reflected 792 baptisms and 558 burials. In addition to the church — begun in the 1740's and completed in 1755 — there were several other buildings. The Indian pueblo, two rows of stone huts and jacales, was enclosed by a wall and had 200 residents. The fields were irrigated, and the mission owned 310 horses, 610 head of cattle, and 2200 sheep and goats.

In 1794 the mission Concepción was secularized. The walls of its church are almost four feet thick; between stone facings they are filled with adobe and small stones. According to the San Antonio Archdiocese, the church "has never fallen into ruins and is today substantially the same church it was over two hundred years ago; and hence it is the oldest unchanged and unrestored edifice of its kind, not only in Texas, but in the United States."

Concepción was one of the missions moved to San Antonio from East Texas in 1731.

An arcade connects the church and offices at the Mission Concepción.

Palm trees and a well occupy the courtyard of the Mission Concepción.

San Francisco Mission Was Moved to San Antonio

By 1730 the East Texas missions were almost dormant. There was not a single Indian at Concepción, San Francisco, or San José. Peace had been made with France, removing that threat to Texas. The viceroy, deciding the presidio Nuestra Señora de los Dolores was no longer needed, closed it.

Because of the Indians' unresponsiveness and the lack of military protection, the Franciscans asked that Concepción, San Francisco, and San José de los Nazonis be moved. The first two missions kept the ecclesiastical part of their names when they settled at San Antonio on March 5, 1731. Since there was already one Mission San José, the Nazonis mission was re-named San Juan Capistrano. The original East Texas mission became San Francisco de la Espada.

Indians were brought from the Frio and Nueces rivers to the three new missions. There were 137 Indians at Espada by 1737, 80 having been baptized; on June 7 all deserted. The missionaries said fear of Apache raids caused them to leave, but the soldiers claimed the Franciscans had mistreated them. In spite of efforts to bring the Indians back, only seven had returned by November. A hundred more arrived in January. Some were killed and some captured by the Apache while gathering fruit on the Medina in 1738. A priest and a number of Indians died in a 1739 epidemic, and the population dropped to fifty.

By 1740 about 120 Indians were in residence at Espada mission, and permanent buildings were begun as the mission prospered. Baptisms totaled 815 by 1762, and there had been 513 burials, an indication of the high death rate. The neophytes occupied three rows of stone huts. Livestock included 145 horses, 1,200 head of cattle, and 4,000 sheep and goats.

At Espada, Father Bartolme Garcia wrote his manual of the Coahuiltecan language.

By 1778, Espada was in decline. There were 133 neophytes and 4,000 head of stock, but the mission was subject to Lipan and Comanche attacks. The church was ruined.

The governor suggested, in 1781, that Espada be closed and its Indians sent to San José. But the mission was still functioning when it was secularized in April, 1794. At secularization movable property was distributed among the Indians, and the fifteen male residents each received about ten acres of land. A hundred acres was given the Indians in common.

Father Francis Bouchu was assigned to Espada in 1858, when only the front and back walls of the church were still standing. Heusinger said of Father Bouchu's forty-nine years there, "With his own hands he built up the side walls on their old foundations, plastered and whitewashed them, put in a wooden floor, hung doors on the entrances, and covered the building with a tin roof."

The roof had to be replaced after an 1883 storm. A restoration was completed in 1911 and again in 1962. Franciscans were once more assigned to Espada in 1967.

The Mission San Francisco de la Espada is the original East Texas mission transplanted to San Antonio.

San Juan Honors the Warrior Saint

On July 10, 1716, Domingo Ramón founded Mission San José de los Nazonis on Bill's Creek, Nacogdoches County, to serve the Nadaco as well as the Nazoni, in whose village it was located. Father Benito Sánchez was in charge of the mission. Ramón wrote the viceroy about the needs of the missionaries; crops could not be raised immediately, and there was no Christian population from which offerings might be expected. Ramón told of the difficult journey. Of the sixty-four oxen brought from Saltillo, four hundred leagues away, only thirty-four remained alive and able to work.

Two years after the 1719 French invasion that caused its abandonment, the Marquis de Aguayo reopened the mission. Before three hundred Indians, he gave a silver headed cane — the usual symbol of office — to the Nazoni chief who had been named governor.

The Indians did not congregate as promised, so San José was moved to San Antonio in 1731. Its new name, to avoid confusion with the Mission San José y San Miguel de Aguayo, was San Juan Capistrano, honoring the crusader St. John of Capistrano who saved Belgrade from infidels in 1456.

The removal from East Texas required over a month. The chapel furnishings, tools, and herds of cattle, horses, mules and burros were brought some three hundred miles. A large group of Indians accompanied the priests. At the new site, fields were cleared and buildings constructed. Supplies from San Juan Bautista sustained the mission population until crops were harvested.

Apache raids were frequent in the first decade. Once, after proposing a peace treaty, Apache warriors, within sight of the settlements, butchered two soldiers who were accompanying them. The soldiers' bones were left behind, the Apache having carried away the flesh to — as Father Vergara put it — "Satisfy their vengeful appetite." Two San Juan Capistrano women were Apache victims. Many neophytes fled the missions. Few would venture into the fields. By late 1737 only about twenty Indians remained. The other 180 had run off. The priests had a hard time getting them to return. A 1739 epidemic reduced San Juan's population from 218 to 66.

By 1745 conditions had improved. Baptisms totaled 515, and 163 neophytes lived in the pueblo. A small stone building housed the Franciscans. Mass was said in a large building made of brush, plastered with mud, and roofed with straw. The irrigated fields produced corn, beans, and melons.

San Juan had 1,000 head of cattle, 3,500 sheep and goats, and 100 horses in 1762. There had been 847 baptisms, and 203 neophytes were in residence near the close of the decade. But decline began and only a dozen families remained at secularization in 1794.

The church was usually the last mission structure built. Mass could be said in the chapel during the early years while building was confined to living quarters, granaries, and storehouses. San Juan's church, begun in the 1760's, was never finished. The chapel which now serves as a parish church was completed in 1756 and restored in 1907.

When the Mission San José de los Nazonis was moved to the San Antonio River it became the Mission San Juan Capistrano.

Espada Has a 230-Year Old Aqueduct

The three East Texas missions were located on the San Antonio River for the same reason the other missions had been built there. Irrigation was required since the rainfall was inadequate for farming.

The friars at San Francisco de Espada soon realized they had made a bad choice of land. The mission's crops were dependent upon gravity flow irrigation, but the river bed adjoining Espada was lower than the mission's fields.

The Franciscans and Indians, in 1740, began building a dam, ditch, and aqueduct to bring water to their fields from a higher point on the river about two miles distant.

The 270 foot dam, curved the wrong way and spanning the San Antonio River, was built of rocks, gravel, and brush. According to tradition, goat's milk was mixed into the mortar to make it waterproof. Over a period of time minerals and soil in the water reinforced the dam. The water ran by ditch to Piedras Creek, which it passed over by aqueduct. The system was completed by 1745, and has continued in use ever since.

The dam was repaired in 1895 by the Espada Ditch Company, and the San Antonio Conservation Society bought the adjacent land in 1941. The United States Department of the Interior designated the aqueduct as a national historic landmark in 1965.

A dam, ditch, and aqueduct were built to serve the Mission San Francisco de la Espada. Still in use, the aqueduct can be seen from San Antonio's Mission Drive.

The Goliad Mission Was Moved from La Vaca Bay

Although La Salle had probably landed there only by mistake, thirty-three years later Spaniards still considered Matagorda Bay particularly desired by the French. In May, 1719, the viceroy received royal orders stating, "On this bay you will cause a fort to be erected on the same spot where M. de la Salle established his in the past."

A few days later a tiny French invasion emptied East Texas. In 1720 the Marquis de San Miguel de Aguayo was ordered to re-establish the East Texas missions. From the Rio Grande, in December, he sent José Domingo Ramón, with forty men, to protect Matagorda Bay from France, with whom Spain was at war. Aguayo reopened the missions and presidios, founded new ones, and returned to San Antonio in January, 1722, after many hardships. Extremely cold weather killed all but fifty of his four thousand horses and all but one hundred of his eight hundred mules.

With horses brought from Mexico, Aguayo started for Matagorda Bay, where construction was begun in April on the fort, which was octagonal and surrounded by a moat. As the foundation was dug, pieces of guns, nails, and other debris from La Salle's fort were found. The presidio was named Nuestra Señora de Loreto.

Father Augustín Patrón had talked to Coco, Cujame, and Karankawa, and many Indians were waiting to enter the new mission when Aguayo arrived. On April 10, 1722, the Mission Nuestra Señora del Espíritu Santo de Zuñiga was founded about two miles from the presidio. Trouble with the neophytes cost the life of presidio commander José Domingo Ramón. The Indians left and refused to return. After four years the mission and presidio were moved about twenty-five miles inland to the Guadalupe near present Victoria.

For ten years the soldiers and missionaries tried to carry out an order to build an irrigation dam. No crops could be planted in that time, and both mission and presidio depended upon supplies brought 230 miles from the Rio Grande, or 150 miles from San Antonio. For awhile after work ceased on the dam, crops grown without irrigation were abundant.

In 1747, four hundred Tamique and Aranama Indians were living at the mission. Most had been baptized. Because the climate was unhealthy and irrigation impossible the mission and presidio were relocated on the San Antonio River near present Goliad in late 1749.

The mission Indians numbered 178 in 1758. They lived in jacales, brush and clay houses with thatched roofs. A stone church and friary had been built. The mission herds included 3200 branded cattle, 120 horses, and 1600 sheep.

There was fear of an English invasion after a British ship was wrecked near Matagorda Bay in 1762. The French and Indian War was in progress and France was Spain's ally. The Apache had begun coming into the mission, abusing the missionaries, and stealing. The neophytes resolved that missionaries who could not defend themselves offered little protection from the Apache. Only ninety-three Indians remained by 1767, and the mission ceased to be active in 1794.

The La Bahía Mission was moved twice before coming to rest a mile south of Goliad on U.S. 77A, where restoration is now in progress.

Ybarbo Settled Nacogdoches Without Consent

After the Marquis de Rubí recommended the abandonment of East Texas, citizens were ordered to move to San Antonio or the Rio Grande. France had ceded Louisiana to Spain in 1764 so there was no further need to occupy the area. Antonio Gil Ybarbo, whose name was really Gil y Barbo, was then living at Los Adaes, where he had been born in 1729. Los Adaes, near modern Robeline, Louisiana, was then the capital of Texas. Ybarbo, a trader and rancher, was the leader of the people in the area.

At Los Adaes the governor, Baron de Ripperdá, announced that everyone had to leave in five days. Land, improvements, and a great deal of personal property had to be left behind. The short notice permitted only slight preparation.

Ripperdá went on to San Antonio, leaving an aged army officer in charge. The move began on July 25, 1773. Lt. José Gonzáles, the commander, and two of the women died at Nacogdoches. Ten children were dead by the time the Brazos was crossed. After two months the refugees arrived at San Antonio, where they were told to settle. They refused. The land offered was partly occupied, and they had no tools or money with which to begin farming.

Ybarbo asked that the Adaesanos be allowed to return to Los Ais, which was close enough to Los Adaes to permit recovery of their tools and other movable property. They were destitute. Thirty had died in San Antonio. Others begged and stole to stay alive. In early 1774 Ybarbo and Gil Flores went to Mexico City to ask the viceroy's permission to move. Otherwise, Ybarbo predicted, the French would pour into the abandoned East Texas.

Surprisingly, Viceroy Bucareli granted the Adaesanos' request. But Hugo Oconór, who had been ad interim governor, objected, and Bucareli reversed himself. Oconór charged that Ybarbo was only trying to resume illegal trading with the French.

The viceroy ordered Ripperdá to settle Ybarbo's people temporarily at least 263 miles from Natchitoches. Ripperdá understood the Adaesanos' plight so he let them settle as far eastward as the order permitted. The new location, on the Trinity River, was named Nuestra Señora del Pilar de Bucareli. Before leaving San Antonio the Adaesanos were organized as a pueblo with Ybarbo in charge. Some did not have enough money to move but planned to follow. The others left in August, 1774.

Ybarbo brought supplies from Los Adaes. Within a short time Bucareli was on its feet. By 1777 the population was 347. The settlement was to be temporary until the viceroy designated a permanent location.

Comanche raids began in May, 1778. Ybarbo, realizing Bucareli could not defend itself, asked to move eastward. Settlement among the Hasinai would give them protection. Some of the settlers went ahead. The Trinity flooded. Before the government answered, in the spring of 1779, Ybarbo led his people to the abandoned Guadalupe mission where the old buildings provided shelter. Nacogdoches — the Pueblo de Nuestra Señora del Pilar de Nacogdoches — was founded.

A furniture and hardware store at 317 Main Street, Nacogdoches, occupies Antonio Gil Ybarbo's homesite.

Ybarbo Built the Stone Fort

In legend, an old Caddo chief living on the Sabine River had twin sons, Natchitoches and Nacogdoches. Natchitoches had black eyes and straight black hair. Nacogdoches was yellow-haired and had blue eyes. On his deathbed the old chief gave the sons an injunction. As soon as the father was dead Natchitoches was to travel three days to the east. There he was to settle his wife and children and begin his tribe. Nacogdoches was to journey three days toward the sunset. His tribe would live in that place. The twin tribes, a hundred miles apart, would be close enough to trade but sufficiently separated to avoid friction. The trail between the Nacogdoche and Natchitoches later became part of the Camino Real.

The Nacogdoche were one of the nine major tribes of the Hasinai confederacy. At their main village, in 1716, the Franciscans founded Mission Nuestra Señora de Guadalupe de los Nacogdoche. The mission was abandoned in 1718 when French soldiers invaded a mission defended by a flock of chickens. Guadalupe was re-established in 1721 and ceased to operate about 1773 when East Texas was vacated. Antonio Gil Ybarbo and the Adaesanos came in 1779.

Although Ybarbo had violated the viceroy's instructions, he was forgiven and made captain of militia and lieutenant governor of the Eastern Province of the New Philippines. He wrote Nacogdoches' first code of ordinances in 1780. To provide the space he needed, Ybarbo erected the building called the Stone Fort in modern times. He kept military and other supplies there; part of the building was used as a jail.

Some Spanish officials had long been critical of Ybarbo, accusing him of trading with foreigners, which was illegal. In a 1792 investigation he was removed from office and sent to San Antonio. He was eventually acquitted but was not allowed to return to Nacogdoches. Two years after his first wife died, in 1794, Ybarbo remarried in San Antonio. He was permitted to move to Louisiana in 1802, but then he returned to Nacogdoches. Apparently the Spaniards simply ignored his violation of exile. Ybarbo died at his home, Rancho de Lucana, on the Attoyac River in 1809.

The Stone Fort was the scene of many historic events. It was torn down in 1902 to make way for a drug store, then rebuilt from the original stones, at the high school in 1907. In 1936 the Stone Fort was again reconstructed on the Stephen F. Austin State University campus.

Peter Ellis Bean was imprisoned in the Stone Fort at Nacogdoches after the death of Philip Nolan.

Philip Nolan Traded in Mustangs

According to the 1794 Nacogdoches census, "Don Felipe Nolan, Irish, native of Belfast, bachelor, 23 years of age; has a negro slave, native of New Orleans, 25 years old...." The same Philip Nolan would be killed by Spanish troops in 1801, at which time he was either mustanging, as he claimed, or plotting to seize Texas, as he also claimed.

Spanish law forbade the entry of foreigners and made trading with them an offense. But in 1780 a royal order made an exception; since horses were in short supply there, Louisiana citizens might buy them in Texas. This was important to traders, for in a barter society horse buyers had to bring goods to exchange. One observer said of Nolan, "His mode of carrying such articles as he takes out is in little barrels which are placed upon pack horses, three barrels on a horse; and in this manner he will travel for hundreds — I may say thousands of miles — through the woods, bartering with the Indians, as he goes along, and receiving in return skins and furs or wild horses."

Nolan was a protege of James Wilkinson, the commanding general of the United States Army, who was also a Spanish secret agent. Although he was in their service, the Spaniards knew Wilkinson was not to be trusted. Their suspicions extended to Nolan.

On Nolan's first Texas trading venture, in 1791, he was arrested and his merchandise confiscated. Five years later he wrote Wilkinson from New Orleans after his third trip. He brought out 250 Texas horses which he sold at Frankfort, Kentucky, and at Natchez.

Nolan was in San Antonio in 1797 with a passport showing that he was buying horses for the Louisiana government. He had brought $7,000 worth of trade goods. Nolan offered to make for Texas' commanding general, Pedro de Nava, a map of the country between San Antonio and Louisiana. Nolan knew the terrain better than the Spaniards did, which made Nava uneasy. Nava ordered Nolan's permanent expulsion.

On June 24, 1798, Vice President Thomas Jefferson — whose curiosity about the country beyond the Mississippi resulted in the Lewis and Clark expedition — wrote Nolan asking about mustangs. Nolan may have talked to Jefferson later, which, if known, would have increased Spanish suspicions.

In August, 1800, Nava ordered Nolan's arrest if he returned. He was to be questioned about his recent activities and his relationship with General Wilkinson, who called Nolan, "a child of my own raising." Without a passport, Nolan came into Texas in 1800. His mustanging company included eighteen Americans, seven Spaniards, and two Negroes. Nolan avoided Nacogdoches, the usual place of entry.

From Nacogdoches, on March 4, 1801, 120 Spanish soldiers went in search of Nolan. Finding his party camped in present Hill County on March 21, the commander demanded Nolan's surrender. A battle ensued and Nolan was killed. Some of the survivors, including Ellis P. Bean, were imprisoned in the Nacogdoches Stone Fort. The first of their trials was held in June, 1801.

Nolan's ears were cut off, presented to the governor at San Antonio, then forwarded to the commanding general at Chihuahua.

Irish-born Philip Nolan, whose knowledge of Texas worried the Spaniards, was killed by Spanish troops near Blum, Hill County, in 1801.

Aury Was a Privateer

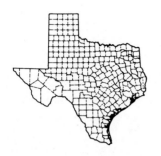

Louis-Michel Aury, born in Paris about 1788, was apparently a French navy deserter. After a few years aboard privateers he was able to purchase his own ships.

The distinction between pirate and privateer was a narrow one. Both used privately owned ships, but the privateer had a commission from some government to prey upon its enemy's ships. The privateer, his vessels and men, augmented the naval power of the belligerent issuing the commission. The pirate was simply a seagoing highwayman. For one whose livelihood was robbing ships, it was desirable to be a privateer. And there was no dearth of governments anxious to issue letters of marque.

Aury had won reknown in the revolution of New Granada, a vice-royalty that became Ecuador, Colombia, Panama, and Venezuela. In 1816 Aury joined a New Orleans group interested in promoting a Texas invasion in support of Mexico's revolt against Spain. The New Orleans backers expected a handsome profit.

Aury intended to establish himself at Matagorda, but its entrance was too easily blocked; so he continued on to Galveston, capturing several vessels on the way. Unfortunately Aury tried to enter Galveston Bay without a pilot. He lost all but two of the captured vessels as they ran aground on sandbars.

Aury put his men to work salvaging cargoes from the wrecked ships, thus angering them. They had expected to go to New Orleans, where spoils would be divided and there were places to spend it. Instead they were doing hard work in the middle of nowhere.

On the night of September 7 there was a mutiny. Some of the two hundred mutineers entered Aury's house, shot him, captured his officers, and set the prisoners from the prize vessels free. The mutineers took everything of value and left for Santo Domingo on three of Aury's ships.

Two days after the mutiny José Manuel de Herrera reached Galveston, supported by the New Orleans group. He took possession of Galveston in the name of the Mexican Republic.

Operating under a commission from that revolutionary government, Aury's ships captured and looted Spanish vessels. The cargoes were sold through New Orleans.

From Galveston Aury wrote his sister in France about the three bullet wounds he received in the mutiny and added, ". . . so that I am now civil and military governor of the province of Texas." Aury left Galveston April 7, 1817 to take the Francisco Xavier Mina filibustering expedition to the Mexican coast. Upon returning he found that Jean Lafitte had taken over Galveston Island.

After a period of maneuvering to stay outside Lafitte's clutches, Aury went back to South America to campaign against the Spaniards. He seized Old Providence Island in 1818, and the justice of the peace there reported Aury's death on August 30, 1821.

A concrete block Humble Oil building, power lines, and a crane occupy the campsite of the privateer Louis-Michel Aury on Water Street in Galveston.

Lafitte Operated from Galveston

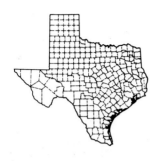

Pierre and Jean Lafitte were natives of Bayonne, France, sons of a French father and Spanish mother. Pierre was born in 1776, Jean in 1780 or 1781. The Lafitte family came first to Hispañola and then, about 1804, to New Orleans.

One or both of the brothers owned a blacksmith shop in New Orleans before they began representing pirates, privateers, and smugglers in disposing of their booty. In time the Lafittes became leaders of the several hundred renegades gathered on Barataria Bay about forty miles southeast of New Orleans. (In *Don Quixote* Sancho Panza was made Governor of Barataria, a name which meant deception.)

Most privateers had commissions from the French during the Napoleonic wars or from governments revolting against Spain. During the war of 1812, privateers were commissioned by the United States. The privateers preyed on Spanish and English shipping. Captured vessels and cargo poured into New Orleans by way of Barataria. Residents of New Orleans had never been unfriendly toward privateers, who supplied fine merchandise at bargain prices.

Governor Claiborne tried to stop the Barataria operation, but he had very little support. Through the Baratarians the best wine could be had for a dollar a gallon. In November, 1813, governor Claiborne offered a reward of $500 for the capture of Jean Lafitte. On the following day Lafitte circulated handbills announcing a reward of $1000 for Governor Claiborne. The Lafittes were seen frequently in New Orleans, until on July 8, 1814, Pierre Lafitte was arrested there by a United States marshal.

The British, preparing to invade Louisiana, were anxious to have the help of the five hundred Baratarians and their four well-equipped schooners. Furthermore, Barataria was well located for an invasion of New Orleans. Whoever held New Orleans controlled commerce on the Mississippi. The British thought their possession of the river might cause the western territory to desert the United States.

After receiving British overtures, Lafitte wrote Claiborne, tendering his services to Louisiana: "I am the stray sheep, wishing to return to the sheepfold." He hoped he and his brother would be given amnesty for helping to defend New Orleans. Pierre Lafitte had escaped from jail, but Jean did not then know it.

Claiborne refused. Army and navy units, with General Andrew Jackson's knowledge, descended upon Barataria and scattered the inhabitants. But instead of causing them to leave the area, to Governor Claiborne's dismay most of the Baratarians moved into New Orleans.

When the British invasion was imminent, the Baratarians joined the defenders. Jackson's army had muskets but no flints with which to fire them. The Lafittes furnished "7500 flints . . . and if it had not been for this providential aid," Jackson said, "the country must have fallen." In 1815 President Madison proclaimed a general amnesty for the Baratarians.

During the next six years the Lafittes were involved in a number of filibustering expeditions against New Spain. Harris Warren said, "Their vessels under various captains

Ruins of a later building stand on the site of Maison Rouge, Jean Lafitte's Galveston house.

sailed as privateers. They themselves preferred to stay in New Orleans or at Galveston. Contrary to popular belief, they were not inveterate mariners. With promises of payment from Spain they betrayed the filibusters. Their vessels preyed upon the commerce of all nations whose merchantmen ventured into the Gulf of Mexico. Captured cargoes of slaves were smuggled into the United States under their supervision . . . . the brothers Lafitte were the royal family of contemporary racketeers.''

Pierre Lafitte was one of the New Orleans group interested in supporting filibustering into Spanish territory, but in late 1815 the Lafittes became Spanish secret agents. Spain was to pay for their services and forgive their crimes.

In March, 1817, Jean Lafitte sailed to Galveston. Mina's army was about to invade Mexico and Aury was providing transportation. Upon his return Aury planned to move his headquarters to Matagorda. On the day after Aury left, Jean Lafitte seized Galveston and appointed a government. He returned to New Orleans where he devised a plan to capture Aury's ships, stopping them from preying on Spanish vessels, enriching himself to the extent of the captured ships and their cargoes, and cutting off supplies to Mina. The plan was never effected.

For awhile Pierre stayed at Galveston. He wrote Jean to send supplies from New Orleans, particularly sulphur ointment for a bad case of itch he had developed. After Jean Lafitte returned to Galveston in September, 1817, he made his settlement, Campeche, headquarters for privateering and smuggling.

When Dr. James Long first invaded Texas, he sought Jean Lafitte's aid. Jean did not commit himself; all the other filibusters had failed. But Pierre, who always made their decisions, thought they should cooperate with Long's republic, probably to keep the Spanish informed on the movements of the filibusters. On October 9, 1819, Long appointed Jean Lafitte Governor of Galveston. Seventeen days later Long fled before Spanish troops. When Long returned, he found Jean Lafitte abandoning Galveston. The Spaniards had refused to have any more to do with the Lafittes and the United States had decided to suppress the pirate stronghold.

In the spring of 1820 Jean Lafitte moved his privateering activities to Mujeres Island, off the Yucatan coast. He died in 1826. Pierre lived in New Orleans until his death about 1841.

Jean and Pierre Lafitte harassed Spanish shipping for years before they became secret agents for Spain.

Jane Long Operated a Richmond Hotel

James Long, who led the last filibustering expedition into Spanish Texas, was born in 1793 in Culpepper County, Virginia. He lived in Kentucky and Tennessee before joining the army as a surgeon. After the end of the War of 1812 he moved to Natchez, Mississippi. He married, on May 14, 1815, Jane Herbert Wilkinson, a kinsman of General James Wilkinson. Long practiced medicine, operated a plantation, and became a merchant.

When the Adams-Oñis Treaty was signed February 22, 1819, many Americans living in the west were outraged. The agreement defined the border between the United States and New Spain as proceeding along the Sabine from its mouth to the 32nd parallel and then directly north to the Red River. James Long and others objected to this renunciation of the American claim to Texas, which they believed had been included in the Louisiana Purchase.

Opponents of the treaty called a protest meeting at Natchez in May, 1819, and decided upon an invasion of Texas. James Long was given command of the expedition, and some $500,000 was pledged to its support. Those who joined Long's army were promised a league of Texas land.

Long reached Nacogdoches on June 21. A provisional government was set up with a twenty-one member council at its head. Long was elected president of the council and given command of the army of the new republic, whose independence was announced on June 23.

The Council promised each soldier 6,400 acres. It ordered a survey of land on the Red River, priced it from 12½¢ to 50¢ an acre, and set up a system of headrights. The new government hoped to populate the country rapidly by a generous disposition of land it did not own. The promise of free land attracted new recruits; Long's force numbered about three hundred men.

Long offered to commission Jean Lafitte a privateer of the new republic. The Lafitte brothers, Spanish secret agents, agreed to assist Long, to betray him to Spain. On October 9 the council authorized a fort to be built at Bolivar Point on Galveston Bay and made Jean Lafitte governor of Galveston.

General Joaquín de Arredondo, ordered to expel the invaders, sent Colonel Ignacio Pérez, and 550 men from San Antonio on September 27. By the time Pérez reached Nacogdoches, Long and the others had fled. The preceding eight years of invasions and expeditions had left Texas devastated and almost without settlers. Except for Indians there were no more than 4,000 people in the province.

Long returned in 1820. He arrived at Galveston April 6 in time to see Jean Lafitte's departure. The Spanish would have no further dealings with him, and the United States had ordered the Galveston robbers' roost evacuated. Long sent word for his men to report to Bolivar Point by April 10. In the meantime he went to New Orleans for money and supplies.

The Council started meeting again on June 4, agreeing to ignore the disruption caused by the Spanish Army in the preceding year. They elected E.W. Ripley president at a salary of $25,000 a year. Ripley accepted by letter but remained in New Orleans,

Jane Long, widowed for sixty years, died at Richmond, Fort Bend County.

pleading the pressures of other business.

After several months at the Bolivar Point fort, on September 19, 1821, Long and 52 men started for La Bahía. The La Bahía presidio and town were taken without a fight. Governor Martínez sent Perez again, and on October 8 Long surrendered. Long was finally sent to Mexico City where he was killed, April 8, 1822, supposedly by accident, shortly after his release from prison.

Jane Wilkinson Long had joined her husband at Bolivar Point in 1820. He refused to let her go with him to La Bahía, so she waited for him at the fort. After Long's capture the men who had remained at Bolivar Point departed. Mrs. Long, her infant daughter, and her black servant, Kiamatia, were alone. On December 21, 1821, her daughter, Mary James, became-probably-the first child of Anglo-American ancestry born in Texas.

The following March she was rescued. She learned of her husband's death in July. After awhile in the United States she moved to San Felipe in 1824, the same year her daughter, Mary James, died.

Jane Long ran a hotel in Brazoria, where William Barret Travis was a frequent guest. When Austin returned from his long confinement in Mexico, a dinner and ball were held in his honor at Mrs. Long's inn September 8, 1835. She made a set of buckskins for Austin. She opened a hotel in Richmond in 1837; M.B. Lamar, who lived there for several months, wrote accounts of the experiences of Jane Long and her husband.

Kiamatia, or Kian, spent her life in Mrs. Long's service. Her granddaughter, also named Kian worked for Mrs. Long after emancipation.

On her plantation two miles from Richmond, Jane Long died on December 30, 1880.

Jane Long was one of the first women from the United States to live in Texas.

Moses Austin Traveled the Camino Real

Settlement of Texas by Americans grew out of Moses Austin's financial reverses in Missouri. Austin always made big plans, usually set in new country. It was perhaps natural, after having lost everything in what had been Spanish Upper Louisiana, that he seek to recover his fortunes on another Spanish frontier.

Austin was born at Durham, Connecticut in October, 1761. After some lead mining experience in Virginia he learned of promising lead deposits in Missouri, then Spanish territory. He moved there in 1798. The village which grew up near Austin's mining operation was named Potosi for a great Bolivian silver mine. After a series of business difficulties, a general depression, and the panic of 1819, Austin decided to settle in Texas.

He traveled to Little Rock to see his son, Stephen F. Austin, then an Arkansas district judge, and left for Bexar in November, 1820, taking a horse, a mule, and Richmond, a black servant belonging to his son. From a point west of Natchitoches, Louisiana, he followed the Camino Real, reaching San Antonio December 23. The Camino Real, the King's Highway, or Old San Antonio Road, had its origins in a trail blazed in 1691 by the first provincial governor, Domingo Terán de los Rios, from the capital, Monclova, to the Mission San Francisco de los Tejas in present Houston County. As additional missions were founded in Texas and Louisiana, the Camino Real was extended to the vicinity of Natchitoches. The Camino Real, measuring 540 miles from the Rio Grande to the Sabine, was the main thoroughfare for settlers at a time when a road's principal virtue was that it indicate accurately the places where creeks and rivers might be crossed with minimum risk to life and property.

Moses Austin was questioned closely by a feeble Spanish administration which was terrified of foreigners. When Austin told Governor Antonio María Martínez he wished to settle three hundred families, the governor ordered him to leave San Antonio "instantly and the province as soon as he could get out of it."

Fortunately, as Moses Austin left the governor's office he met Felipe Neri, the Baron de Bastrop, an old acquaintance. The Baron persuaded Martínez to see Austin again. A few days later, by reason of the Baron's influence, Martínez forwarded — with his recommendation that it be approved — Austin's request to bring in colonists.

Austin left Texas by the Camino Real. According to Austin family tradition he was robbed and deserted by a traveling companion. Austin and Richmond subsisted on roots and acorns as they tried to make it to a settlement. The exhausted servant had to be left with settlers at the Sabine River. Austin was so ill and weak from the hardships of the trip that he was confined to bed for three weeks. Moses Austin died June 10, 1821.

A ROYAL HIGHWAY - EL CAMINO REAL
THE OLD SAN ANTONIO ROAD
BLAZED IN 1691 BY DOMINGO TERAN DE LOS RIOS
THE FIRST PROVINCIAL GOVERNOR OF TEXAS
SO EXPRESSED AND ORDERED BY THE KING OF SPAIN

The Camino Real, the King's Highway, and the Old San Antonio Road were names given the route connecting settlements on the Rio Grande and the East Texas missions.

Stephen Austin Carried Out His Father's Plan

While Moses Austin was in Texas, Stephen F. Austin left Little Rock, apparently having given up the judgeship. He wrote from New Orleans, "I offered to hire myself out as a clerk, as an overseer, or anything else, but business is too dull here to get into business. There are hundreds of young men who are glad to work for their board." Fortunately Joseph H. Hawkins agreed to teach him law and pay him a small salary.

But Spain had granted the Austin colonization request, and Stephen F. Austin went to Texas to make arrangements in behalf of his father. En route to San Antonio he learned that Moses Austin had died June 10.

Governor Antonio Martínez authorized Stephen Austin to explore the country along the Colorado. There were then only three settlements in Texas. San Antonio and Goliad together had 2,516 residents. The Nacogdoches population was twenty.

Austin's first settlers arrived near present Washington in November, 1821. Austin went to Mexico City to get confirmation of his grant. He had to be sure the new Mexican government would honor the Spanish grant and would accept him as Moses Austin's successor. He spent a year in Mexico.

Austin was the executive, judicial, legislative, and military head of the colony. Since neither he nor his colonists were familiar with Mexican law, Austin wrote a short civil and criminal code in 1824 that was substantially the only law in the colony until 1828.

Austin was by far the most successful of the empresarios. An 1831 census showed a population of 5,665 in his colonies. The Austin settlements were peaceful and productive, due largely to his care in selecting colonists. He required references and expelled a few undesirables. Austin's settlers were not the adventurers so common to the frontiers, but men wanting homes.

Austin said of his work, "The prosperity of Texas has been the object of my labors, the idol of my existence — it has assumed the character of a religion, for the guidance of my thoughts and actions, for fifteen years." Two months before his death Austin wrote, "I have no house, not a roof in all Texas that I can call my own. The only one I had was burned at San Felipe during the late invasion of the enemy." Worn out by his labors, Austin died December 27, 1836, at the age of forty-three years.

Evaluating the Austins' work, George P. Garrison stated, "Of all the men who have figured in American history there are no other two who have attracted so little attention from their contemporaries and have yet done things of such vast and manifest importance, as Moses Austin and his son Stephen . . . . The student will scarcely need to be reminded of the series of mighty effects, increasing in geometrical ratio in magnitude and historical significance, that followed directly thereform. Thus it runs: the Texas Revolution, the annexation of Texas, the Mexican War, and the acquisition of the Southwest below the forty-second parallel from the Rio Grande to the Pacific — a territory almost equal in extent to the Louisiana Purchase and which contains the bulk of the mineral wealth of the United States."

Stephen Fuller Austin devoted himself to the service of Texas until his death a few months after independence was won. His statue is at San Felipe, Austin County.

Jared Groce Brought Ninety Slaves With Him

Jared E. Groce was one of the few wealthy men to come to Texas. Born in Virginia in 1782, Groce lived in Georgia and then owned a large Alabama plantation. When Groce moved, in 1821, more than fifty covered wagons were needed to transport his possessions. He used pontoon bridges to cross the rivers.

Groce settled at the Madelina crossing of the Brazos in present Waller County. Since the system of land distribution provided eighty acres for each of his ninety slaves, Groce received ten sitios. He expanded his land holdings rapidly. In 1822 Groce planted the first cotton in Texas and built the first gin. To defend his plantations he maintained a company of negro Indian fighters. Groce, leading thirty of his black cavalry, joined an 1824 expedition to pacify the Karankawa.

At his plantation, Bernardo, four miles south of present Hempstead, Groce built a large home of cottonwood logs. The gallery, which ran the length of the house, was supported by polished walnut columns. The kitchen was in a separate building, to minimize the fire hazard which cooking constituted. A building referred to as Bachelor Hall was used for entertaining. Quarters for the house servants were nearby. The houses, kitchen, dining hall, and day nursery of the field slaves were located by a lake. Groce's Ferry was at the Bernardo plantation.

In 1833 Jared Groce moved to a Grimes County plantation home. He called it Groce's Retreat since he had fled the malaria along the Brazos. While President David G. Burnet and his cabinet were moving the government from Washington-on-the-Brazos to Harrisburg, they stayed three days at Groce's Retreat in March, 1836.

Groce, crippled in both hands, did not take an active part in the fighting, but he contributed large quantities of supplies to the Texas Army and furnished treatment for sick and wounded soldiers. Sam Houston and the Texas Army camped near Groce's Ferry from March 31 to April 14, 1836, just before the battle of San Jacinto. Bernardo housed refugees from the Runaway Scrape; the women made sandbags and Groce's slaves melted lead water pipes to make bullets for the army.

Groce died November 20, 1836 at Groce's Retreat.

A change in the course of the Brazos left the site of Groce's Ferry, south of Hempstead, Waller County, well away from the river.

Austin's Town Was at a Good Brazos Crossing

Upon his return from Mexico in 1823 Austin found that two districts had been formed in his grant, which lay between the Brazos and Colorado Rivers. An alcalde presided over each district, assisted by a constable. Appeals from the alcalde's courts were to Austin.

Needing a site for his headquarters, which the governor declared would be named San Felipe de Austin, Austin chose the settlement John McFarland had begun in 1823 on a bluff near the Brazos crossing of the Atascosito trail.

In December Austin created the San Felipe district. San Felipe was laid out, Spanish style, around four plazas. Commercio Plaza was on the river, where McFarland's ferry was located. Two blocks farther south was the Military Plaza; soldiers' quarters, an arsenal, and a cemetery were located there.

Austin, who never married, boarded until 1828, when he built a cabin on Bollinger Creek a mile west of the Brazos. He wrote that his house was "a thoroughfare for the whole country" and that he lived poorly, having some "corn coffee, corn bread, milk and butter, and a bachelor's household, which is confusion, dirt, and torment." Austin's house was a double log cabin with two rooms on each side of an open dog trot. One room served as an office and one as living quarters. The mud-chinked cabin, with its stove, chimneys, and fireplaces, cost him $600.

San Felipe consisted of about twenty log houses in 1828; three schools were then in operation. Thomas J. Pilgrim, a teacher and Baptist preacher, said of San Felipe, "that there were some rude and illiterate people among them is no more than may be said of almost any society, and that some were vicious and depraved is equally true. But what there was of evil you saw on the surface for there was no effort at concealment."

The first public function Noah Smithwick attended at San Felipe was the tarring and feathering of a poet who wrote, "The United States, as we understand; Took sick and did vomit the dregs of the land. Her murderers, bankrupts and rogues you see; All congregated in San Felipe."

Austin raised $1,300 to build a college at San Felipe, but the revolution made it impossible. Godwin Brown Cotten published Texas' first newspaper, *The Texas Gazette*, in 1829. Gail Borden, Jr., who later founded the Borden Company, began his *Telegraph and Texas Register* in San Felipe, but moved to Harrisburg as Santa Anna's army approached.

The convention of 1832, the first gathering representing all of Texas, was held in San Felipe. In 1833 another convention drew a constitution for statehood separate from Coahuila, the colonists assuming that the new president, Santa Anna, was sympathetic to their problem of being seven hundred miles from the capital at Saltillo. The Consultation of 1835 met at San Felipe and the provisional government was set up there. As Houston retreated, the citizens burned San Felipe and joined the Runaway Scrape. After San Jacinto, the town was rebuilt. As recently as 1938 a ferry was still the only means of crossing the Brazos at San Felipe.

A well was necessary to the town of San Felipe, Austin County.

Two conventions and the Consultation of 1835 were held in the San Felipe town hall, which was burned, along with the rest of the town, as Santa Anna approached.

Settlers from the southeastern United States hoped for a new life in Austin's colony.

A Mexican Fort Was Captured at Velasco

In November, 1821, Stephen F. Austin's schooner, *The Lively*, landed supplies and eighteen of his first colonists at the mouth of the Brazos River. Some 25,000 immigrants entered Texas there in the next fifteen years. The traffic brought Velasco into existence and made it an important town.

In time the heavy immigration of Americans aroused the concern of the Mexican government. The result was the law of April 6, 1830, which was an attempt to cut off settlement from the United States and stimulate colonization by Mexicans and Europeans. The law established customhouses and forts.

The Velasco fort was located on the Brazos about 150 feet from the seashore. A stockade had been built by driving posts into the ground in two concentric circles. The six-foot space between the two rows of posts was filled with sand. A moat surrounded the outer wall. On a high mound at the center of the enclosure was a nine-pound cannon that could be fired over the stockade walls in any direction. The fort accommodated the customhouse and 120 soldiers.

Settlers resented establishment of the fort for several reasons, one of which was because it facilitated the collection of duties on imports and exports. The duties were sometimes quite high and always burdensome. The fort was subordinate to the Anahuac commander, Colonel John Davis Bradburn, originally from Kentucky. Bradburn had been with Francisco Xavier Mina in his 1817 invasion of Mexico.

Bradburn took charge of the Anahuac garrison in November, 1830, and set about making enemies. He arrested the Mexican commissioner and surveyor charged with issuing land patents, delaying settlers in receiving titles. Bradburn used slaves without compensating owners and let his soldiers abuse the settlers. He closed all the ports except Anahuac and dissolved the council at Liberty.

After Bradburn arrested Patrick Jack, Edwin Waller, and William Barret Travis in May, 1832, John Austin and others forced Bradburn to promise the prisoners freedom; he did not keep his promise. On June 13 the settlers adopted the Turtle Bayou Resolutions declaring their grievances against Bradburn and the Bustamante government.

John Austin returned to Brazoria, got a cannon to use against Bradburn, and started down the Brazos with it. The commander of the Velasco fort, Domingo de Ugartechea, tried to stop the vessel carrying the cannon. Between 100 and 150 armed settlers surrounded the fort on the evening of June 25. The battle lasted all night, and in mid-morning the Mexicans surrendered.

Ten settlers were killed and eleven wounded. Of the Mexican garrison, the casualties were five dead and sixteen injured. A few days later Bradburn's resignation was forced by José de las Piedras, the Nacogdoches commandant. The first blood had been shed in Texas over differences between settlers and the government.

The Battle of Velasco, the first clash between Texas colonists and the government at Mexico City, was fought near Highway 332 in present Freeport, Brazoria County.

Daniel Parker Founded Pilgrim Church

In 1832, Daniel Parker attempted to found a Primitive Baptist Church in Texas. Unable to do so, since the Roman Catholic Church was established by law, he organized a church in Illinois and brought its thirty-six members to Anderson County. Parker pastored Pilgrim Church at Elkhart — which is probably the oldest Protestant church in Texas — until his death December 3, 1844, at the age of 63. Parker was a delegate to the Consultation and was elected to the Texas Congress, although ministers were not permitted to serve.

Eight other Primitive Baptist churches were organized under Pilgrim's auspices. Pilgrim church was an important civilizing influence. Minutes of the church meetings reflect Pilgrim's struggle to maintain itself and have an effect on the society. Its rules of decorum provided for an inquiry into his "caracter" when any man was absent "three meatings hand running." Periodically there was a foot washing ceremony. At least a dozen years before emancipation, slaves and freedmen were accepted as members of Pilgrim Church.

Some members judged themselves harshly. In February, 1850, "Brother Mead ... made Some statements relative to a charge against him for attending a ball and stated that if any of the Bretherens feelings was hurt he was sorry for it. After proper acknowledgements he was forgiven." A few months later, "Brother Mead informed the church he had got angry on the day of the Election the 5 of August 1850 for which he was Sorry. the church frely forgive him." One member decided he was beyond help and urged action against himself: "Brother Garrett request the church to throw him overboard as was Jonah, so the church by her vote excluded Brother Garrett."

Sins of the flesh threatened church and community. After a committee had called to "labour" with him, Brother G. H. addressed the male members of the church. They "advised him to desist and put away a Certain Woman he had Liveing at his house and he Refusing so to do," the committee was ordered to labour further. After a few months the committee reported that Brother G. H. was straightened out.

A double standard obtained in Anderson County. An 1849 committee reported, "Sister K. N. has had an illegitimate child ... and says that I. J. is the father of it." Both were excluded from the church, "for the violation of the rules of decorum in pointed contradiction as well as the crime of illegitemacy against K. N." In the following year Mrs. K. N. unsuccessfully applied for restoration, but Brother I. J. was readmitted a few months later.

Brother P. Q. had charges brought against him in 1865 for "writing letters and corresponding with a lady on an improper Subject ...." The committee laboured with P. Q., who admitted guilt and was following no occupation to support his family. On the committee's recommendation, P. Q. was excluded.

Brother Jasper Starr was excluded for "Joining what he calls the Christian Church."

In 1852 the church received as a member "Brother Quarley a Colerd Man belonging to John Davis." A few months later the church asked for Brother Quarley's freedom, so he could preach.

Apparently the most vexatious problem was when two women members had a falling

The Pilgrim Baptist Church at Elkhart, Anderson County, was probably the first Protestant congregation in Texas.

out. Sister H. and Sister C. were charged with fighting. In February, 1866, the church "took up the case of our two colored sisters for fighting and contradicting of each other . . . ." Sister C. was excluded. Charges against H. were dropped.

A more prolonged disagreement arose between Sisters V. W. and X. Y. A committee was appointed and several sessions were required in analyzing the controversy. Apparently the church fathers never really understood what the quarrel was about or who was at fault. They simply got tired of both parties.

The committee found that, "sis V. W. says that sister X. Y. told her that she had a conversation with Bro. Ben Parker Relative to some Reports in Circulation and he, Ben Parker, said she ought to have Contradicted said Reports and sister X. Y. Denies Making any such Statements and in the 2nd place sister V. W. says she told sister X. Y. about said Reports being in Circulation about her some time in the Spring of 1866 which sister X. Y. Denies."

For three more months the case dragged on. Attempts to pacify the belligerent ladies failed, so there was no alternative to a church trial. Probably neither realized how thin the patience of the congregation had worn. ". . .the case was divided and sister V. W. was Put on trial and stood three to exclude and five to Retain and the Manority Contended They was Right whereupon a motion was made to Reconsider the vote and the vote was then Reconsidered and Brother Hendryx withdrew his Request for a Division of the case and the vote was then taken jointly and the Church says by her vote that Sisters X. Y. and V. W. is no longer members of her Body. there being no other business, adjourned in Peace."

Early Texas churches were no more sumptuous than the homes of their members, as the Pilgrim Church replica demonstrates.

Vice President Anderson Died at the Fanthorp Inn

Henry Fanthorp, a native of England, came to Texas about 1832. He was a forty-two year old widower when he filed for land in the Austin and Williams colony.

In 1834, Fanthorp built a home for his new bride, Rachael Kennard, where the Houston and Springfield mail route crossed the road connecting Nacogdoches and San Felipe. Because of its location many people needing lodging and board stopped by Fanthorp's house, a situation that created many early Texas inns.

A man was expected to feed and take in anyone who happened to be passing. If he called his place an inn he could charge for bed and board. Otherwise, travelers imposed upon him as if he owed them something. One lady Texan wrote, "We became very weary of entertaining people of whom we knew nothing; but there was no hotel nor house of any kind where they could go . . . ." On one cold night she and her husband slept on the floor while ungrateful strangers occupied their bed. She said, "We are told to take in the stranger as by so doing we 'may entertain an angel unawares.' I do not think that class of guest often traveled in Texas. . . ."

Henry Fanthorp's house quickly become Fanthorp Inn. The first post office in the county was established there in 1835, with Fanthorp as postmaster. In 1837, he opened the first store in the county. Fanthorp called the town which developed Alta Mira.

Kenneth Anderson, a North Carolinian, had come to San Augustine in 1837. He was collector of customs, then speaker of the House, and vice president of the Republic. He died at the Fanthorp Inn July 3, 1845. Alta Mira became Anderson in his honor; Anderson County is named for him also.

The Fanthorp Inn, at Anderson, Grimes County, was located at a well-traveled intersection.

Robertson Founded Nashville-on-the-Brazos

Hearing of Austin's colony some Nashville, Tennessee, businessmen began their own Texas project. Sam Houston and Sterling Robertson were members of the company which was formed in February, 1822, to found a colony. By the time Austin reached Mexico City to have his grant confirmed, the agent for the Nashville group, Robert Leftwich, had made his application.

On April 15, 1825, Leftwich was given permission to locate eight hundred families in Texas. Leftwich then assigned the contract to the Nashville company, and Sterling and Felix Robertson were sent to explore the grant. While his cousin reported to their partners, Sterling Robertson remained in Texas. Born in Tennessee in 1785, Robertson had grown up in Nashville and served in the army at the Battle of New Orleans.

In 1827 the area granted to the Nashville group was enlarged to a hundred miles by two hundred miles; except for Austin's grant it was the largest made to any empresario. Colonization was delayed two years because of disagreements within the company. Austin, who had helped Leftwich obtain the grant, was anxious that the Nashville company be successful. The tract adjoined the Austin colony and, when populated, would be a buffer against the Indians. For five years there was no settlement in the grant. Just as colonization was about to begin, the law of April 6, 1830 prohibited further immigration from the United States.

Austin and his agent, Samuel Williams — believing Mexico was about to give the Nashville grant to a French company — asked for and received a contract on the land.

In 1834, the governor at Saltillo cancelled the Austin-Williams grant and declared Sterling Robertson the empresario. Robertson founded Sarahville de Viesca and then, in 1835, Nashville-on-the-Brazos, which became the headquarters of Robertson's Colony. Nashville was one of the sites under consideration to be the capital of the Republic. It was the seat of Milam County from 1837 to 1846, but went into decline after the county government moved to Cameron. The post office closed in 1868.

Just prior to the revolution, in 1835, the colony was returned to Austin and Williams. Robertson was a delegate to the 1836 convention, a signer of the Declaration of Independence, and during the revolution he raised a company for army service. He was a member of the First Texas Congress.

Robertson, in 1837, filed suit to clarify his empresario rights, but he died at Nashville on March 4, 1842, five years before his claim was upheld by the courts.

A stone on U.S. 79 in Milam County marks the site of Nashville-on-the-Brazos, the capital of Robertson's Colony.

Santa Anna Overwhelmed the Alamo

After San Antonio fell to the Texans on December 10, 1835, Santa Anna's brother-in-law Martín Perfecto de Cós and his troops were paroled to Mexico on their pledges not to participate further in any attack on Texas.

In the meantime Santa Anna, "with the fires of patriotism in my heart and dominated by a noble ambition to save my country," was headed for Texas with some 6,000 troops. Frank Johnson and a handful of others were at the Alamo holding San Antonio. The Alamo was a walled enclosure with a ruined church, the remains of the Mission San Antonio de Valero. Probably most of the citizens had forgotten about its mission origins, as had Santa Anna, who called it "a solid fortress erected by the Spaniards."

The Texan leadership was divided. General Sam Houston sent Jim Bowie to destroy the Alamo and retreat; Governor Henry Smith had William Barret Travis reinforce it. When Santa Anna arrived on February 23, Bowie and Travis had joint command of about 150 men. Santa Anna's surrender demand was refused, and the Alamo siege began on the 24th. Travis, because of Bowie's illness, took full command. He made an appeal for help to "the People of Texas and all Americans in the world."

On March 1, thirty-two Gonzales men arrived. James Bonham was sent to get Fannin and his army. He returned alone. Travis had 182 men and some eighteen cannon.

By March 4, all of Santa Anna's troops had arrived. Later he wrote, "I felt that a delay would only hinder us and ordered an immediate attack." He gave his final orders on the afternoon of the 5th.

Early the next morning, with some 4,000 troops in readiness, one long bugle note was sounded, then the deguello, the "fire and death" call, giving notice that no prisoners would be taken. The infantry advanced carrying scaling ladders; cavalry was ranked behind to cut down the foot soldiers if they faltered. Cós, in spite of his pledge, commanded one column.

The Mexicans, too many to count, stormed the outer walls, then pursued the defenders into the buildings. The battle was over within an hour. Santa Anna wrote, "The filibusters, as was their plan, defended themselves relentlessly. Not one soldier showed signs of desiring to surrender, and with fierceness and valor, they died fighting .... We suffered more than a thousand dead or wounded, but when the battle was over, not a single man in the Alamo was left alive."

Mrs. Almeron Dickenson, her child, Travis' Negro servant, Joe, and Mrs. Horace Alsbury were among the survivors, all non-combatants, slaves, women, and children. Francisco Ruiz, San Antonio's alcalde, who came to attend the wounded, reported that the bodies of the 182 defenders were piled in heaps and burned.

The men who died at the Alamo fighting for restoration of the Mexican constitution of 1824, did not know that Texas independence had been declared at Washington-on-the-Brazos on March 2. They took a heavy toll of the Mexican army, gave the rest of Texas time to prepare for Santa Anna, and taught that it was for all Texans as it had been for them, "God and Texas — Victory or Death."

The Cenotaph, in front of the Alamo, honors those who fell there March 6, 1836.

Fannin Surrendered at the Coleto

James Walker Fannin, Jr., was born in Georgia in 1804. After two years at West Point he withdrew. In 1834 he brought his family to Velasco, where he traded in slaves. He was captain of the Brazos Guards at Gonzales on October 2, 1835, as the revolution began, and he was one of Austin's scouts as the Texans moved on San Antonio. He led Texas troops in the Battle of Concepción on October 28.

Houston made Fannin a colonel in December. Fannin began assembling a force to attack Matamoras. When he learned that General José Urrea had fortified Matamoras he moved his troops to Goliad. Around the presidio Nuestra Señora de Loreto the town of La Bahía had grown up; in 1829 the legislature at Saltillo changed its name to Goliad.

Copano, forty miles away, had been used as a port of entry by General Martín Perfecto de Cós before the siege of San Antonio. By holding Goliad Fannin could cut off supplies to San Antonio coming by water through Copano. But Santa Anna, unwilling to rely on that port, was bringing his supplies overland with the army.

As Santa Anna advanced toward San Antonio, General Urrea moved toward San Patricio. Meanwhile Fannin was improving the fortifications at the presidio.

From the Alamo Travis sent James Bonham to get Fannin's help on February 19, but Fannin remained at Goliad. Travis' second call came February 25, and Fannin, with 320 men, started to San Antonio. But Fannin changed his mind and resumed work on what he called "Fort Defiance."

On March 3, Houston sent orders for Fannin to go to the aid of Travis; then learning, on March 11, of the fall of the Alamo he told Fannin to retreat to Victoria. Fannin got the order to retreat on the 13th, but he waited on the return of small parties he had sent out on various errands, using up supplies and splitting his forces. Meanwhile, Urrea was headed for Goliad.

On the 18th Fannin remained at the fort while some of his men wasted horses and ammunition in useless sparring with Urrea's advance elements. The oxen were left unfed, so that they were weak and hard to control as he moved his army out the following morning. Fannin's retreat was under the cover of fog. The party moved slowly because of the weakened oxen, the only means of pulling the supply wagons. An ammunition cart broke down. While the Texans were repairing it or transferring its cargo, Mexican troops surrounded them.

After fighting the rest of the day on the open prairie and suffering sixty casualties, Fannin surrendered the following morning. By that time Urrea had brought up his artillery; he had about a thousand effective troops. Fannin's men were imprisoned at Goliad.

Near Goliad Fannin's army fought the Battle of the Coleto and surrendered to General José Urrea.

The Goliad Prisoners Were Executed as Pirates

Santa Anna tried to discourage American volunteers to the rebel cause by a decree stating that foreigners coming into any part of Mexico "armed and for the purpose of attacking our territory shall be treated and punished as pirates. . . ." Most of Fannin's men had been in Texas only a few weeks. Fannin probably surrendered unconditionally — the only alternative was a fight to the death — but he let his men believe they would be paroled. They were confined in the presidio church.

Herman Ehrenberg wrote:

"As prisoners we were stuffed into the old church for the night, literally stuffed, as we stood so close man to man that it was impossible at the highest for only one fourth to sit down. It was well that the inner room of the church had a height of thirty-five to forty feet. If it had been lower we would have suffocated."

"The first night of our captivity passed away in discomfort. A burning thirst tormented us, and although we asked repeatedly for water, we had to wait until eight o'clock in the morning before six of our men were allowed to go to the river and get water for themselves and the other prisoners. We drank great quantities of water and refreshed our parched throats, but now that we had satisfied our thirst we began to feel very hungry and waited impatiently for the moment when we might leave the prison to get our rations. Our hopes were vain; there was no water in the evening, and another dreadful night came upon us. The heat had become much greater, and was much more stifling than during the preceding night. Several of my comrades were so exhausted that they slept standing, for the crowded state of the prison prevented us from lying down."

The next morning the prisoners received water and some meat but, "it was raw and we had no way of cooking it. We gathered pieces of wood which lay scattered on the floor, stripped the walls of their woodwork; and soon several of our comrades who always knew what to do in an emergency had kindled two fires. But the fires had to be very small, as our heat and thirst were by that time almost unendurable and only a few men at a time could roast their meat; the night was over before we had finished our cooking. Those of us who stood farthest from the fire gave up the idea of cooking the meat and ate it raw. . . ."

Urrea, who had gone on to Victoria, urged clemency, but Santa Anna on March 23 sent orders to execute the prisoners. On the 27th they were divided into groups and marched away in three different directions. About a mile from the fort each group was halted and the guards began shooting. Fannin and about forty other wounded prisoners were killed in the fort. Some 342 prisoners were executed; they were burned as the Alamo defenders were, a layer of bodies being alternated with a layer of wood.

Twenty-eight prisoners escaped. Twenty were spared because of their usefulness as physicians or mechanics and through the kind intervention of Francisca Alvarez, the wife of one of General Urrea's officers.

Fannin and his men spent a great deal of time making improvements to the old La Bahía presidio at Goliad. (Television reception was then no problem.)

James Walker Fannin, Jr., a West Pointer, was a colonel of the Texas Volunteers.

Fannin and his men were brought back to the La Bahía presidio after their surrender.

The Goliad Prisoners Were Buried in a Common Grave

The American reaction to the Goliad execution was immediate and bitter. Until then interest in the Texas revolution had been slight, but the execution of United States citizens without trial was barbarous. The stories told by survivors concerning the surrender terms compounded the outrage. They claimed that Urrea had offered paroles to induce them to lay down their arms and then had not paroled them. Probably Fannin misrepresented the terms of the surrender, perhaps thinking Urrea's request for clemency might be effective or simply believing it best that his men not know what was in store for them. Nevertheless, public sentiment in the United States hardened against Mexico.

The massacred prisoners were stacked in ricks and burned; officials in the Texas government planned to inter the remains at the first opportunity. On June 3, 1836, General Thomas Jefferson Rusk and troops of the Texas Army gathered the charred remains together, gave them a military funeral, and buried them in a common grave.

In the 1850's the grave was marked by a pile of rocks. The area was grazed by large herds of wild cattle — earlier the mission Espíritu Santo had some 40,000 head — and the stones were scattered as time passed.

In 1885 a monument to the memory of the prisoners was erected in the town of Goliad, since no one knew the location of the grave. Later the site was fixed by Clarence R. Wharton and others by reference to bone fragments found on the ground and an earlier designation by Dr. Joseph Barnard, a survivor of the Goliad Massacre.

As a part of the centennial observance in 1936 the present monument was constructed. Its inscription, after referring to the circumstances of death of the Goliad prisoners, reads, "Beneath this monument reposes their charred remains. Remember Goliad!"

During the Texas Centennial observance a monument was dedicated at the grave of the Goliad prisoners near Fannin, Texas.

Dilue Harris Was in the Runaway Scrape

Dilue Rose was born in St. Louis in 1835. Her father, Dr. Pleasant W. Rose, brought his family to Texas in 1833 and located at Stafford's Point. She married Ira A. Harris in 1839. They lived in Houston until 1845 when they moved to Columbus. She died at Eagle Lake April 2, 1914.

Mrs. Harris' reminiscences provide an excellent contemporary account of the Runaway Scrape, the general exodus of settlers as Santa Anna brought his armies east of San Antonio. Spanish generals were accustomed to depopulating Texas whenever the central government's control had been threatened. Mexican generals would probably behave no differently, the settlers reasoned. And Santa Anna, who had been the hope of believers in constitutional government, had shown himself to be a tyrant without compassion.

The Runaway Scrape began in January, 1836. As Mexican armies assembled on the Rio Grande, Texans of American origin began leaving for Louisiana. This movement grew during the siege of the Alamo, for it was obvious that Travis could not hold out. As some families departed, the hazard of Indian attack increased for those who remained, and they soon followed their neighbors.

Sam Houston, finally receiving effective command of the army, reached Gonzales on March 11. Upon learning of the Alamo's fall he ordered a retreat, hoping to build up his 374 man army. The Runaway Scrape became a stampede as new areas were exposed to Santa Anna and the people pondered the fate of the Alamo defenders. Families abandoned everything not easily moved, and made for the Sabine.

Dilue Harris said, "Then began the horror of the Runaway Scrape. We left home at sunset, hauling clothes, bedding, and provisions on the sleigh with one yoke of oxen. Mother and I were walking, she with an infant in her arms. Brother drove the oxen, and my two little sisters rode in the sleigh."

When the Harrises reached the San Jacinto River, "There were fully 5,000 people at the ferry . . . . Every one was trying to cross first, and it was almost a riot." Her sister died and was buried at Liberty. The Rose family had been on the road five weeks when a rider told them of Houston's victory at San Jacinto. Mrs. Harris said, "The first time that mother laughed after the death of my little sister was at his description of General Houston's helping to get a cannon out of the bog."

Dr. Rose then turned back toward home, stopping at the San Jacinto battleground. "We were glad to leave the battlefield, for it was a gruesome sight. We camped that night on the prairie, and could hear the wolves howl and bark as they devoured the dead."

Dilue Harris' house stands at the corner of Bowie and Washington in Columbus, Colorado County.

The Armies Camped Opposite Each Other at Columbus

At Gonzales, Houston learned of the Alamo's fall. He led his army toward the Colorado River on March 13, 1836, ordering Gonzales residents to follow; the town was put to the torch so it would be of no value to Santa Anna. Houston's army numbered less than four hundred men. By retreating into the most populous part of Texas he could add volunteers and be close to supplies.

Houston reached Burnham's crossing on the 17th. The army had grown by some two hundred men. Two days later he crossed the Colorado and moved down to Beason's Ford, near Columbus, which had been founded in 1823 by Austin colonists, probably on an Indian village site. There he camped for several days.

General Joaquin Sesma, on his way from San Antonio to Anahuac, reached the Colorado on the 21st. His 725 soldiers camped two miles above Houston's location. For five days the armies remained in place as the Texas force increased to some 1200. Houston considered attacking Sesma, then changed his mind and continued his retreat on the 26th, ordering Columbus burned.

Houston's withdrawal toward the Brazos and news of Fannin's surrender caused renewed panic. It had been assumed that the Colorado was the easternmost point of retreat. Disgusted with Houston's decision, men deserted the Texas army in droves to take care of families who were now vulnerable to the Mexican armies. Houston reached San Felipe on the 28th.

Santa Anna overtook and joined Sesma near Columbus. They reached San Felipe's ruins on April 7. The Runaway Scrape reached its peak as Santa Anna crossed the Colorado and news of Goliad spread. W. B. Dewees, of Columbus, wrote: "...now you might behold children falling from the wagons which still kept on, leaving the children behind . . . all seemed to look out for themselves alone. . . ."

There were no bridges and few ferries. Spring rains overflowed the rivers. The San Jacinto was too swift to cross by raft. Dewees said, "But thanks to the invention of two Yankees, the difficulty was soon obviated. They proposed that we should look us out a couple of very tall pine trees, so that their length might be sufficient to reach across the river, cut them down, peel the bark from them and then lay them across the river so near to each other that we might place the wagons on them and pull them across the river with a rope. This we did, upon each loaded wagon we placed a number of women and children, the 75 wagons were all drawn over in the course of half a day."

After the victory at San Jacinto many refugees did not go home immediately. When Dewees returned to his farm he learned that there were no settlers west of the Colorado. He hired two men to stay with him and help defend against Indians. Because of the disruptions of the Runaway Scrape, fields were neglected and very little food was raised. The armies had taken all of the stores and frightened away all the game. Dewees wrote, "...some of us have tried to raise a late crop of corn by planting in June, but this experiment has not succeeded well. What we are to do I know not, but I trust some way will be provided for us. . . ."

Santa Anna's advancing armies camped in what is now a residential area of Columbus.

Deaf Smith Was the Texas Spy

Erastus Smith was born April 19, 1787, in New York. He lived in Mississippi before coming to San Antonio in 1821. His health had been bad, but he recovered — except for his hearing — after awhile in Texas. He married Guadalupe Ruiz Duran in 1822.

Because of his wanderings Smith knew the country around San Antonio better than anyone else. He took no part in the revolution until Mexican troops refused to let him enter San Antonio, where he lived. He then joined Austin, who had Bexar under siege.

Smith was with James W. Fannin and James Bowie at the battle of Concepción October 28, 1835, and guided Texas troops into San Antonio. He then took his family to Columbia and joined Houston at Gonzales.

In March, 1836, Houston sent Smith to San Antonio to get details of the Alamo siege. When Smith returned he brought Mrs. Almeron Dickenson, her baby, Angelina, and Travis' negro servant, Joe. Mrs. Dickenson had been taken before Santa Anna after the Alamo fell. The Mexican dictator had held Angelina, given Mrs. Dickenson a horse and servant, and asked that she convey his compliments to Sam Houston. She was to warn Houston that all who opposed Santa Anna would share the fate of those at the Alamo. Only rebels who laid down their arms immediately might be spared.

When Houston led his army out of Gonzales, Deaf Smith followed with a squad to guard the refugees. Gonzales had been burned. At dawn on the following morning the refugees were startled by explosions in the town; Smith's men were only blowing up poisoned liquor that angry citizens had left for the invaders.

On April 18 Houston's army reached Buffalo Bayou opposite Harrisburg, which had been burned by Santa Anna. Deaf Smith swam the bayou and brought in two Mexican prisoners, a scout and a courier. Houston got valuable information from them on Santa Anna's location and the condition of his army.

The next morning Houston started after Santa Anna. Smith and Henry Karnes were continually scouting ahead of the army. On the day before the San Jacinto battle Smith and Sidney Sherman captured a ferry-boat load of Mexican flour. The grateful soldiers made dough, which they cooked on sticks.

On the 21st Houston handed Smith two axes and told him to destroy Vince's bridge, which would keep General Vicente Filisola from reinforcing Santa Anna. Smith dispatched the bridge and returned in time to take part in the Battle of San Jacinto.

When the Congress of the Republic honored its soldiers, Smith received special attention. He was to have his pick of any public "house and lot in the city of Bexar" except "forts, courthouses, calabooses, churches, and public squares." Houston ordered Smith to sit for a portrait. Not long after the painting was done Smith died at Richmond, November 30, 1837.

Deaf Smith is buried at Richmond, Fort Bend County.

Houston Took It All at San Jacinto

From Gonzales, on March 13, 1836, Houston and his 374 men began to retreat eastward. In the next five weeks the Texas Army grew, and Houston waited for the appropriate time to fight. President David G. Burnet and the government were furious. They were hard put to stay out of Santa Anna's clutches. Although Burnet ordered Houston to fight, the retreat continued.

Once during the retreat a soldier, S. F. Sparks, invited Houston to lunch on some chickens Sparks had acquired without purchase. As Houston started to eat, General Rusk said, "General Houston, it is a maxim in law that he who partakes of stolen property knowing it to be such is guilty with the thief." Houston answered, "No one wants any of your law phrases." Then he told Sparks, "I'll not punish you for this offense, but if you are guilty of it the second time I will double the punishment."

On April 17 Houston changed course and headed toward the coast. The next day he learned that Santa Anna's army had crossed Vince's Bridge and would have to return the same way. Houston took his men across Buffalo Bayou on the 19th. There was minor action on the 20th.

When there was no attack the morning of the 21st, soldiers in both armies assumed there would be no battle. Martín Perfecto de Cós' army crossed Vince's Bridge, bringing Santa Anna's strength to about 1300 men. Deaf Smith was sent to destroy the bridge and was told to hurry back if he wanted to participate in the battle.

At 3:30 in the afternoon Houston lined up his men in a single rank. He led them across the open prairie toward Santa Anna's camp, about three quarters of a mile distant; they were some two hundred yards away at 4:30 and had not been discovered.

Then Houston ordered the attack. Shouting "Remember the Alamo! Remember Goliad!" the Texans came down on the surprised Mexican camp; it was the siesta hour. The battle lasted eighteen minutes. Six hundred and thirty Mexicans were killed and 730 taken prisoner. Of Houston's 783 men, nine were killed or mortally wounded. Thirty others were injured, including Houston, who was shot in the ankle.

Santa Anna, in a private's uniform, was recognized the following day when fellow prisoners greeted him as "El Presidente." After Houston demanded that the Mexican armies be withdrawn beyond the Colorado prior to negotiations, Santa Anna wrote General Vicente Filisola, "The small division under my immediate command having had an unfortunate encounter yesterday afternoon, I find myself a prisoner of war. . . ."

Texas was independent, a fact Mexican politicians would not admit. After nine years as a Republic, during which time Mexico made no real effort to reclaim it, Texas became part of the United States. Mexico chose to consider the annexation an act of war, and in the campaign which followed, the United States acquired New Mexico, Arizona, Nevada, California, Utah, and parts of Colorado, Wyoming, Kansas, and Oklahoma. The San Jacinto victory eventually resulted in the addition of nearly a million square miles, almost a third of the present continental United States.

The San Jacinto Monument, in Harris County, was dedicated in 1936 by Texans celebrating a hundred years of independence.

Noah T. Byars Brought the Convention to Washington

Washington-on-the-Brazos developed as a result of the ferry Andrew Robinson began operating in 1822 at the La Bahía Road crossing of the Brazos. Robinson, Austin's first settler, had arrived in the preceding June and camped on the Washington site. Robinson opened a hotel in 1830. His son-in-law, John W. Hall, laid out a town, but the first residence was not built until 1833. The town was probably named for Washington, Georgia, the home of one of the developers.

Just prior to the revolution Washington's population was about one hundred; however, it was important enough to have been selected as the site of the 1835 Consultation. After fighting began at Gonzales the Consultation was moved to San Felipe, where Texas' only printing press was located; printing facilities would be important to any government established by the delegates.

The Consultation at San Felipe set up a provisional government for Texas as a state — separate from Coahuila — of Mexico. It was hoped that grievances might still be adjusted and that Texas could remain part of Mexico. The provisional government consisted of Governor Henry Smith, Lt. Governor James W. Robinson, and a council representing each municipality. In January, 1836, the council asked municipalities to send delegates to a convention which would meet March 1 and consider the question of independence.

John Hall and other businessmen insisted that the convention be held at Washington since the Consultation had been taken away. They promised to furnish a suitable meeting place without cost, an important — perhaps the decisive — consideration to a government without funds.

Noah T. Byars, a South Carolinian, who had opened a blacksmith shop in Washington a few months before, offered his partially completed building. On February 18, eight individuals and business firms contracted to pay Byars and his partner, Peter M. Mercer, $170 for three months' use of the structure, which was to be completed prior to March 1. The building was still unfinished when the Convention met, to the discomfort of delegates. The Washington businessmen did not pay Byars the rental agreed upon.

Byars served as an armorer during the revolution. In 1841 he was ordained as a Baptist preacher. He established about sixty churches, mostly on the frontier, and died in Brownwood in 1888.

Near a bend in the river Andrew Robinson located his ferry, the beginning of Washington-on-the-Brazos.

The Texans Declared Their Independence

As the Independence Convention met at Washington-on-the-Brazos the Alamo defenders were besieged by some 5,000 Mexican troops; another of Santa Anna's armies was proceeding along the coastal plain, and Texans were leaving for Louisiana in numbers that increased every day. Stephen F. Austin and the other Texas representatives had attempted without success to raise money in the United States. No one wanted to finance a civil war; chances of repayment were too slight. But if Texas were independent, some lenders might be willing to gamble.

For the delegates, there was really no alternative to a declaration of independence unless they moved across the Sabine, as Santa Anna seemed to desire. They met March 1 in Noah T. Byars' building. A norther had dropped the temperature to 33°, and the hall was, according to observer William Fairfax Gray, "an unfinished house, without doors or windows. In lieu of glass, cotton cloth was stretched across the windows, which partially excluded the cold wind."

George Childress called the meeting to order, and the permanent chairman appointed a five man committee to draft a declaration of independence. Childress was chairman, serving with Collin McKinney, James Gaines, Bailey Hardeman, and — the only one of the five not to have a county named for him — Edward Conrad. The document submitted to the convention on the following day was mainly the work of Childress, who probably wrote it before arriving at Washington. After the declaration was put before the convention, only Sam Houston spoke on the question of its acceptance. The fifty-nine delegates, without dissent, adopted it within less than an hour. A constitution was drafted and a temporary government set up. Because of reports of advancing Mexican armies the convention adjourned on March 17, and Washington-on-the-Brazos was evacuated three days later. Robert Hamilton and George Childress were sent to the United States to seek recognition of the new republic.

George Childress, thirty-two years old, had moved to Texas from Tennessee only a few weeks before his election to the convention. His mission to the United States was unsuccessful. In the next five years he tried repeatedly to establish himself as a lawyer in Texas but was unable to do so. In June, 1841, he wrote President Lamar asking for employment. At Galveston, on October 6, he committed suicide with a bowie knife.

Dr. Ashbel Smith, the physician who attended Childress, asked why he had inflicted the six wounds. Childress answered, "It is the effect of an oversensitive mind. I had neither money to bring my wife to this country nor to enable me to visit her." He died three hours later.

Noah T. Byars rented an unfinished hall, of which this is a replica, to businessmen who wanted the Independence Convention to meet in Washington-on-the-Brazos.

Treaties of Peace Were Signed at Velasco

At Velasco, where *The Lively* had landed eighteen of Austin's first colonists, and where the first blood had been shed over differences between Texans and the government of Mexico, Santa Anna confirmed the independence of Texas.

President David G. Burnet and his ad interim government had remained on the move since his election on March 16, 1836. After the San Jacinto victory the government was no longer a fugitive but Burnet's life was no less difficult. There was no public treasury. Volunteers from the United States — arriving to fight in a war that was already concluded — constituted a threat to public order.

On May 14, Burnet and Santa Anna signed two treaties of peace. The public treaty, among its ten articles, provided that Santa Anna would not again take up arms against Texas, that his troops would be withdrawn beyond the Rio Grande, and that he would be sent home as soon as possible. The secret treaty pledged Santa Anna to try to get Mexican acknowledgement of Texas independence, with the Rio Grande as the boundary.

Although General Vicente Filisola started withdrawing Mexican troops on May 26, the Texas Army, enlarged by recent volunteers from the United States and with nothing better to do, refused to let Santa Anna leave the country. Santa Anna was held prisoner on shipboard at Velasco, where citizens and soldiers clamored for his execution. The Mexican dictator, the "Napoleon of the West," spent much of his time writing haughty letters demanding his release. On May 20, the Mexican government declared void all acts done by Santa Anna while he was a prisoner.

Finally, Santa Anna was spirited away to safety at Columbia one dark night, and Houston got him out of the country on the pretext that he was going to Washington to urge that the United States admit Texas to the Union. Houston did not trust Santa Anna, but he wanted him out of Texas before something happened. As Andrew Jackson warned, Santa Anna's execution would turn world opinion against Texas. Furthermore, Houston knew Santa Anna's talents for trouble-making and preferred that he make it elsewhere. "Restored to his own country," Houston wrote, Santa Anna, "would keep Mexico in commotion for years, and Texas will be safe." Santa Anna was sent to Washington in late November and reached Vera Cruz in February, 1837.

Near the Freeport Coast Guard station the treaties of Velasco were signed.

The Comanche Swept Down on Fort Parker

When Elder Daniel Parker and his Baptist congregation made the first settlement in Anderson County in 1833, four families went on to present Limestone County. There they established Fort Parker in the following year. The outer walls of their cabins formed part of a stockade. Loopholes for firing rifles and elevated blockhouses made it possible for a few settlers to defend the fort against a substantial Indian war party. Each family lived there at the fort but sometimes stayed overnight on its own land, as far as a mile away.

The patriarch of the community was Elder John Parker, 79; he and "Granny" were the parents of Elder Daniel of Pilgrim Church. Among the thirty-eight at the fort were Elder John's sons James, Silas, and Benjamin, James' daughter Rachel Parker Plummer, and the L. D. Nixons, who were in-laws of James Parker.

The people of Fort Parker had joined the Runaway Scrape. Hearing of the San Jacinto victory, they returned to the fort in late April, 1836, and began catching up on the work that had been neglected.

On the morning of May 19, James Parker, Nixon, Plummer, and four others were away from the fort working their land. At about 9 o'clock a party of five to seven hundred Comanche and Kiowa stopped out of rifle range of the fort. Under a white flag, one Comanche came close enough to parley — his mission was probably to evaluate the defenses — and asked for directions to a spring. The Indians wanted to be given a beef also.

Benjamin Parker went out to talk to the Indians and returned saying he thought they intended an attack. Although his brother, Silas, begged him not to go back, Benjamin insisted. Rachel Plummer said, "He started off again to the Indians, and appeared to pay but little attention to what Silas said . . . . When Uncle Benjamin reached the body of Indians, they turned to the right and left and surrounded him . . . . I ran out of the fort, and passing the corner I saw the Indians drive their spears into Benjamin."

Several fled the fort. Silas was killed and scalped trying to protect Rachel Plummer. Samuel and Robert Frost were killed in the fort. Elder John Parker was lanced, as was Granny Parker, who was raped and left for dead. Mrs. John Parker, Mrs. Duty, and Granny Parker died later of their wounds.

Cynthia Ann Parker, nine years old, and John Parker, six years old, the children of Silas, were taken by the Comanche. The other captives were Mrs. Kellogg, Rachel Plummer, and her fifteen-month old son, James Pratt Plummer. The raiding party divided the captives, taking away Mrs. Plummer's child. She never saw him again.

Mrs. Kellogg was sold to Delawares who, in turn, sold her to James Parker at Nacogdoches about six months after her capture. Sam Houston paid the $150 ransom since Parker was without funds.

Rachel Plummer was used as a slave by Comanche women. They tried to make her miscarry since an infant would interfere with her work. Six months after the Fort Parker raid she gave birth to a son. She begged to keep it, but one day some braves took the baby away from her. While others held Mrs. Plummer they threw the child into the air, let

The replica of Fort Parker, Limestone County, follows the general style of the original.

it fall to the ground several times until it appeared to be dead, then pitched it to her. When Mrs. Plummer realized the baby was alive and tried to revive it, a brave knocked her down and put a rope around the baby's neck. He dragged it behind a horse and then "threw the remains into my lap, and I dug a hole in the earth and buried them."

After a year and a half Rachel Plummer was ransomed north of Santa Fe. She reached the home of her father, James Parker, February 19, 1838, and died exactly a year later, not knowing whether her son still lived. John Pratt Plummer was ransomed and arrived home in 1843.

John Parker was said to have become a Comanche brave and was wounded on a raid into Mexico and left behind. The story was that he married a Mexican girl and became a substantial rancher. In fact, John Parker was ransomed, and James Parker brought him back from Fort Gibson, Indian Territory, when he recovered James Pratt Plummer. The *Northern Standard*, at Clarksville, on February 16, 1843, reported that: "Mr. Parker of Montgomery County passed through town during the present week, with a nephew and a grandson, who had been in captivity among the Comanches, and were redeemed by General Taylor at Fort Gibson, last fall, from the Delawares, who purchased them. The grandson is the son of Mrs. Plummer, the narrative of whose captivity has been seen by most of our readers."

By 1843 only Cynthia Ann Parker remained captive. She would be recovered in 1860 by Governor L. S. Ross after almost a quarter century among the Comanche. Her son by Peta Nocona — Quanah Parker — would be the last war chief of the Quahadi Comanche.

—Texas Collection, Baylor University

Cynthia Ann Parker lived with the Comanche for twenty-four years. Her infant child, Prairie Flower, died soon after their return to civilization.

The First Masonic Lodge Met Under an Oak Tree

Stephen F. Austin and six other Masons met at San Felipe in 1828 to consider organizing a lodge, but decided to wait. Seven years would pass before the first dispensation was issued for the founding of a lodge in Texas.

In March, 1835, Anson Jones, John A. Wharton, Asa Brigham, James A. E. Phelps, Alexander Russell, and J. P. Caldwell met at Brazoria to organize the first Masonic Lodge. Jones wrote, "The place of the meeting was back of the town of Brazoria, near the place known as General John Austin's, in a little grove of wild peach or laurel, and which had been selected as a family burying ground by that distinguished soldier and citizen." They met beneath a two hundred year old oak tree.

The application was made to the Grand Lodge of Louisiana. The new lodge would be named for J. H. Holland, at that time the Grand Master of Louisiana. By the time the dispensation was issued, January 27, 1836, Texas had been invaded, and Brazoria was in the path of one of Santa Anna's armies. In February the last meeting of Holland Lodge was held in Brazoria, with James Walker Fannin, Jr., who would be executed at Goliad a few weeks later, serving as the senior deacon. In March Brazoria was abandoned and General Urrea took possession of everything belonging to the lodge.

Jones, who would be the last president of the Republic of Texas, had joined the army. The permanent charter of Holland Lodge was brought from Louisiana and delivered to Jones just before the Battle of San Jacinto, "on the prairie between Groce's place and San Jacinto, while we were on the march." Jones wrote, "Had we been defeated at San Jacinto, Santa Anna would have captured the charter of Holland Lodge, as Urrea had the dispensation at Brazoria." (This would have presented no problem since Santa Anna was a Mason.)

Because of Brazoria's reduced population, Anson Jones convened Holland Lodge at Houston in October, 1837. When the Grand Lodge of Texas was formed, with Sam Houston presiding, Holland Lodge of Houston became Holland Lodge No. 1. The Nacogdoches body became Milam Lodge No. 2, and that at San Augustine, Redland Lodge No. 3.

The land on which the Masonic oak stands was acquired by the Grand Lodge of Texas in 1952. The tree, three centuries old, was in bad shape, necessitating some $500 worth of repairs.

Beneath the Masonic Oak at Brazoria's Pleasant and Wood streets Anson Jones and six other Masons organized the first lodge in Texas.

Houston Was the Second Capital

Augustus and John Allen, brothers from New York, speculated in Texas land for four years before founding Houston. Their Buffalo Bayou site was well chosen; it was necessary to change means of transport, from ship to wagon, at that point.

Naming the town for the victor at San Jacinto, the Allens offered free government building sites if Houston should be made the capital of the republic. Gail and Thomas Borden surveyed and platted the new town. Civil War Governor Francis Lubbock told of trying to find Houston in early 1837 and passing it by without noticing.

Sam Houston, a major booster, wrote in April, 1837, "On the 20th of January a small log cabin and twelve persons were all that distinguished it from the adjacent forests, and now there are upwards of 100 houses finished, and going up rapidly (some of them fine frame buildings) and 1500 people, all actively engaged in their respective pursuits."

The government of the Republic of Texas started business at Columbia in October, 1836. By President Houston's order the capital was located at Houston from April 19, 1837, until Lamar moved it to Austin in October, 1839. During Houston's second term the seat of government was again at Houston for a few months.

One of the best accounts of early Houston was left by Gustav Dresel, a native of Germany. During his first week there he slept on the floor of a friend's office "until the Gerlachs provided sleeping accommodation for me in the attic of their boardinghouse, by the side of thirteen companions. Pigs regularly held a party under the office during the night, so that we had to go to sleep to the melodious grunting of those unbearable animals; the change of lodging was, therefore, not disagreeable."

Houston was a boom town with few women and with many residents living in tents. Trees and stumps covered most of the dedicated streets. A general holiday air prevailed. Much gambling and drinking were accomplished. There were always Indians in town to sell furs; each wanted to see Sam Houston — whose years among the Cherokee were common knowledge — before departing.

The new town had a classless society according to Dresel: "The President, the whole personnel of the government, many lawyers who found ample means of support in these new regions, a large number of gamblers, tradesmen, artisans, former soldiers, adventurers, curious travelers from the United States, about a hundred Mexican prisoners who made suitable servants, daily new troops of Indians — all associated like chums on an equal footing. When fall came with its northers, and there were only three stoves in the whole of Houston, we used to light fires in front of the saloon in the evening, stand around them and enjoy — not excepting the President — hot drinks with merry speeches."

The capitol of the Republic was located on the Rice Hotel site.

Three-Legged Willie Carried the Constitution on His Hip

Georgia-born Robert McAlpin Williamson suffered an illness in his fifteenth year that made him an invalid for two years and crippled the lower part of his right limb; recovering, he strapped it behind him and walked on a wooden leg.

Williamson had a fine mind and read widely during his illness. He was admitted to the Georgia bar when he was eighteen. Williamson fought a duel — which was fatal to his opponent — over a young lady, and when she married another, he came to Texas.

Williamson settled at San Felipe in 1826. For three years he edited *The Cotton Plant*, a newspaper he owned with G. B. Cotten, a portly old bachelor. Noah Smithwick said a man once asked what the G. B. stood for, and Cotten replied, "Damn you, can't you see? Great Big Cotten, of course."

The Cotton Plant went broke. Williamson and Cotten sold the printing press to F. C. Gray who published the short-lived *Texas Republic*. Smithwick wrote, ". . .the editor, F. C. Gray, removed to California where he became wealthy, a circumstance so phenomenal as to unsettle his reason. Gray died in New York by his own hand."

As to Williamson, Smithwick told of being awakened one morning by someone calling from outside, "Oh Smithwick; come here; here's a man with a broken leg." Smithwick said, "Recognizing the voice as that of Judge Williamson, I hastily donned my clothing, and opening the door, found Willie sitting on the step with his wooden leg broken; he had been making a night of it with that result. I took the fractured limb to my shop and braced it up so that it was as good as new, and the Judge went on his way rejoicing." As a result of Williamson's early opposition to Santa Anna, Colonel Ugartechea issued a letter to local officials ordering his arrest. Williamson was a member of the Consultation of 1835, and the provisional government authorized him to raise a ranger company. At San Jacinto Williamson served in the cavalry.

The Congress of the Republic of Texas assembled in joint session on December 16, 1836, and elected Robert M. Williamson judge of the third district and ex officio justice of the Supreme Court. He rode the circuit, holding court where there had never before been a formal administration of justice. In Colorado County, there being no courthouse, he heard cases beneath the huge Columbus oak, whose trunk measures twenty feet around and whose branches spread some 120 feet.

Settlers were not always anxious to have the law brought to their neighborhood. Judge Williamson was as hard as he had to be. Once in a hostile community, he unpacked the law books from his saddle bags, took his place behind a table on which he laid a pistol and rifle, and called, "Hear ye, hear ye, court for the third district is either now in session or somebody's going to get killed."

On another occasion a drunken lawyer was arguing a case when Judge Williamson asked, "Where is the law to support your contention?" The attorney drew a knife and said, "There's the law." The judge pulled his pistol, pointed it at the lawyer, and answered, "Yes, and there's the Constitution."

Three-Legged Willie established respect for the law in a fashion best understood by

Judge Robert M. Williamson held Colorado County's first district court term beneath the Columbus Oak.

frontier people. Smithwick wrote, "Being appointed judge for the district of Washington, which office he filled with credit both to the state and himself, he would leave a courtroom over which he had just presided with all the grace and dignity of a lord chief justice and within an hour be patting Juba for some nimble-footed scapegrace to dance . . . The Judge also conducted revival meetings by way of variety. . . ."

Williamson was a member of the Texas Congress for several years. He believed so strongly in annexation to the United States that he named his son Annexus. Governor Oran Roberts described Williamson at the inauguration of the new state government, "There sat Robert M. Williamson (Three Legged Willie), the fearless, whose bold and incisive oratory gave him power of control, and whose big heart drew to him the affections of all who knew him."

Williamson served in the state senate but was defeated in his congressional race in 1849 and for lieutenant governor two years later. He died in Wharton in 1859. Williamson County is named for him.

—Duncan Robinson

Judge Williamson's trousers had to be made with three legs to accommodate both his maimed right limb and the wooden peg he wore.

Rangers Camped on the Site of Waco

The Waco Indians, a Wichita tribe, came into Texas in the early 1700's. One of their villages was at the site of modern Waco where there was a dependable spring; in 1824, a scout wrote Stephen F. Austin about the quality and coldness of the spring water. Later a band of Cherokee drove the Waco from the site.

Other than a settler named Boyd, who built a house near Waco in 1835 and was burned out, the first white man to take an interest in the Waco site was George B. Erath. A native of Vienna, Austria, Erath began surveying in Texas in 1833. He fought at San Jacinto, then became a member of T. H. Barron's ranger company, which was stationed at the falls of the Brazos.

In early 1837 Barron's men established a fort at the Waco Indian village location. Erath wrote, "We expected to occupy the fort permanently. Waco was in possession of buffalo and only a short time before had been vacated by the Waco Indians; cornstalks were found in the fields they had cultivated, and peach trees were growing where the city now stands. We built some shanties for barracks near the big spring on the river, but only remained there three weeks when an order came from the Secretary of War for us to return to the falls as we were too far out to do them service. We went back, calling the place we had left Fort Fisher." The Republic's Secretary of War was William S. Fisher.

The country around Waco remained unsettled because of Indian troubles. In 1839 Neil McLennan, who was born in Scotland, accompanied Erath on an Indian campaign in the area. He persuaded Erath to return and survey some land for him near Waco, but the Indian troubles were far from over. In August, 1840, Erath scouted the area again and noted, "At Waco village we found ripe peaches on the Indian trees."

In the next years Erath passed through McLennan County on Indian campaigns and surveyed for those who might settle there when the Indian menace was over. Ignoring hostile Indians, Neil McLennan built his house some eight miles from present Waco in 1845. A few years before, his brothers, Laughlin and John, and John's wife were killed by Indians. John McLennan's three children were carried away; Erath told of the recovery of one of them, ". . .John McLennan, junior, afterwards known as 'Bosque John,' was delivered; he had been captured when six years old on Pond Creek, in 1836 . . . . His remaining relatives found him in the garb of an Indian, and it took several years to restore him to the ways of the white man."

Erath surveyed and platted the Waco townsite in 1849. Lots sold for $5 each. The town was to be named Lamartime, for President Lamar, but Erath insisted, successfully, that it be Waco Village. McLennan County's government was located there in 1850.

Waco's modern ranger headquarters and museum were built near an 1837 ranger campsite.

Walter Lane Escaped the Battle Creek Fight

In 1838 W. F. Henderson took a surveying party into the vicinity of present Corsicana to lay out a county. On their way from Franklin they stopped for a day at Parker's Fort, where Cynthia Ann Parker had been taken captive two years before.

One of the men, Holland, disappeared in present Navarro County. The rest of the party became frightened and insisted upon returning to Fort Parker. Buck Barry refused to go, saying he would keep working until Henderson returned with another crew. Henderson found Holland's body about five miles from their last camp, "so much mutilated by the buzzards that we could not tell whether he was scalped or not."

Henderson thought they should go back and get Barry, but the others refused. The party of about a dozen men had only two guns. They reached Fort Parker that night. Two volunteers went with Henderson to warn Barry, but it was too late. Barry had already been killed. The Indians understood that surveying parties meant the advent of settlers. The Navarro County country still had numerous buffalo, and the Indians wanted to keep it closed to whites.

The Battle Creek fight occurred that October. Henderson and Walter P. Lane were members of another party surveying in Navarro County. As they traveled they encountered several small groups of Indians who showed no hostility although they seemed concerned about the surveyors' activities. There were twenty-four men in the surveying crew.

The numbers of Indians increased. About fifty Kickapoo camped nearby warned that seventeen Ioni intended to kill the surveyors. When the attack came the surveying party was on the open prairie. They ran for the cover of nearby timber, but seeing Indians waiting there, the twenty-two men — two had returned to the settlement for equipment — took cover in a ravine. It was about one o'clock in the afternoon. Some three hundred Tehuacana, Ioni, Waco, Caddo, and Kickapoo surrounded them.

By climbing trees, the Indians could fire into the ravine and were picking off the surveyors one by one. The fighting continued until midnight. Several more were killed as they left the ravine beneath a full moon. Henderson, Violet, Barton, and Lane made it to the timber. Violet, badly wounded, could not travel further. He was left in a thicket to be rescued if the others reached safety.

Lane, with a serious leg wound, had to be supported by Henderson and Barton. They were without food and water and their clothes were torn and bloody. Fortunately they met a Kickapoo who took them to Parker's fort. Two other members of the party had escaped also. Violet was brought in, and some fifty men went to the battleground to see if any of the surveyors still lived. There were none. Wolves had stripped the sixteen bodies. The bones were gathered and buried.

Lane, born in Ireland, was a San Jacinto veteran. As a major he fought in the Mexican War and in 1864 he was wounded at the Battle of Mansfield. At the close of the Civil War he was a Confederate brigadier general.

The Battle Creek fight actually occurred on Richland Creek when Kickapoo Indians, realizing that surveyors preceded white settlers, attacked a surveying party near this marker a few miles from Dawson, Navarro County.

Lamar Believed Texas Would Extend to the Pacific

Mirabeau Buonaparte Lamar was born in Georgia in 1798. He was secretary to Governor George Troup, a newspaperman, and a Georgia state senator. After his wife died of tuberculosis and he had failed in two attempts to be elected to Congress he came to Texas.

Arriving in 1835 Lamar became interested in the Texan opposition to Santa Anna. He joined the Texas Army as a private during the retreat eastward. Lamar demonstrated a great deal of courage and ability in the fighting just prior to the battle of San Jacinto. On April 21 he was commissioned as a colonel and given command of the cavalry. Ten days later he was secretary of war of the Republic. In another month he was commander of the Texas Army, with the rank of major general, but difficulties with his men caused him to resign.

In the first election Lamar was made vice president. He was nominated for president by enemies of Sam Houston, who could not succeed himself. Lamar's two opponents, Chief Justice James Collinsworth and former Attorney General Peter Grayson, committed suicide. Collinsworth was drowned and Grayson shot himself, after which Anson Jones — who later died by his own hand — wrote that henceforth, "I shall be surprised at no one's committing suicide. . . ."

When Lamar took office, December 10, 1838, the population of the republic was some 65,000, including slaves and Indians. As president, Lamar urged a system of public education and took a hard line toward the Indians. Receipts during his administration were $1.1 million and expenditures were $4.8 million, causing the currency to depreciate badly.

Lamar dreamed of a Texas that would rival the United States in size and strength. He, of course, opposed annexation, although he later changed his mind and worked for Texas' admission to the union.

One of Lamar's acts to expand the Republic was putting the capital on the frontier; Texas would grow toward and past it, and eventually the Republic would reach the Pacific. When Congress appointed a commission to choose a permanent capital, Lamar suggested that they look at an area in which he had recently hunted. There the commission found two tiny settlements, Waterloo and Montopolis. They were favorably impressed and recommended the site. In the late spring of 1839 the new capital city, Austin, was laid out. A traveler wrote, ". . .Rome itself with all its famous hills could not have surpassed the natural beauty of Waterloo. . . ."

While armed guards watched for Indians the government buildings were begun. The capitol was of logs. In October, forty wagons brought the government records and property to Austin. By the time Austin was six months old the population was 856, composed of 145 slaves, 61 women, 100 children, and 550 men. The records show that seventy-three of the men were church members.

Gambrell wrote, "The Republic of Texas of which he dreamed would spurn annexation to the United States, conquer as much of Mexico as it might want, and contest with the United States for the leadership of the Americas."

Mirabeau Lamar is buried beside his wife at Richmond, Fort Bend County, beneath a stone inscribed "Ex-President of Texas."

At the Neches the Cherokee Were Expelled

Perhaps the most shameful episode in the history of the Republic was the expulsion of the Cherokee from East Texas. One of the civilized tribes, the band that settled in Texas left the southeastern United States earlier than the rest of the Cherokee.

The Texas Cherokee were led by Chief Bowles. He was the son of a Scotch-Irish trader and a Cherokee mother and was born about 1756. Bowles was not Indian in appearance. He had reddish hair, grey eyes, and freckles. He had been a chief for many years before bringing his people to East Texas about 1820.

Not long after coming to Texas — when Chief Bowles was in his late sixties — Richard Fields became the leader of the Texas Cherokee. Additional members of the Cherokee arrived, as well as scatterings of Alabama, Choctaw, Delaware, Kickapoo, Shawnee and others who allied themselves with the East Texas Cherokee.

From the outset the Cherokee were anxious to get title to the land on which they had settled. When Stephen Austin was in Mexico City seeking confirmation of his grant, Cherokee representatives were also trying to get evidence of their ownership. The Cherokee efforts were repeated again and again to Mexican and Texan governments.

Fields, apparently deciding the Mexicans would not confirm the Cherokee title, became involved in the Fredonian rebellion and was tried and executed by the Cherokee in 1827. Bowles again became their leader.

The Consultation of 1835 promised the Cherokee that their boundaries would be defined, and Sam Houston assured them that they would be secure in their holdings in present Cherokee, Van Zandt, Smith, and Rusk counties. But after the war with Santa Anna ended, President Houston could not get the Cherokee land treaty ratified.

In 1838 there was evidence that the Cherokee had been involved in the abortive rebellion of Vicente Cordova. When Lamar became president he acted on the assumption that the Cherokee eventually would have to be moved out of Texas. In May, 1839, Lamar learned of a letter which indicated that the Mexican government would seek Cherokee support against the Republic. Lamar ordered the Cherokee expelled. Some five hundred troops were sent to move them across the Red River.

The Battle of the Neches was fought on July 15 and 16, 1839. The first day's engagement took place in present Henderson County and the second in Van Zandt County. Chief Bowles, then eighty-three years old, led some seven or eight hundred Cherokee warriors. Mounted on a fine sorrel horse and wearing "a sword and sash, and military hat and silk vest," he was killed on the second day.

John Reagan wrote: "When at last the Indians retreated, Chief Bowles was the last one to attempt to leave the battlefield. His horse had been wounded many times and he shot through the thigh. His horse was disabled and could go no further, and he dismounted and started to walk off. He was shot in the back by Henry Conner, afterwards Major Conner; walked forward a little and fell, and then rose to a sitting position facing us, and immediately in front of the company to which I belonged. I

A stone in the pasture of the old Harper Place, east of Ben Wheeler, Van Zandt County, marks the spot where Chief Bowles died at the Battle of the Neches.

had witnessed his dignity and manliness in council, his devotion to his tribe in sustaining their decision for war against his judgment, and his courage in battle, and, wishing to save his life, ran towards him, and, as I approached him from one direction, my captain, Robert Smith, approached him from another, with his pistol drawn. As we got to him, I said, 'Captain don't shoot him,' but as I spoke he fired, shooting the chief in the head, which caused instant death."

When Bowles had seen that his people were losing the battle he had ordered a retreat but remained on the field saying, "I stay. I am an old man. I die here." Smith claimed Chief Bowles' sword, which had been given him by Sam Houston, and some of the participants took his scalp. Within a few days the survivors of the East Texas Cherokee were in the Indian Territory.

Sam Houston, who was in Tennessee at the time, was extremely bitter about the expulsion of the Cherokee and killing of Bowles. Houston had twice lived with, and was an adopted member of, the Cherokee. Upon his return, Houston made a speech at Nacogdoches in which he said that Bowles was a better man than his murderers. Houston's life was threatened and he offended some good friends. When General Burleson sent Chief Bowles' hat to Sam Houston the result was an hour and a half speech by Houston before the Texas Congress attacking Lamar's Indian policy and defending the claims of the Cherokee.

Later Anson Jones wrote in his diary that Sam Houston "is not so strong in what he does himself, as in what his enemies do; it is not his strength, but their weakness — not his wisdom but their folly. Cunning, Indian cunning . . . . Old Bowles . . . learned him all he knows."

Chief Bowles was half Cherokee but resembled his Scotch-Irish ancestors. He was killed in battle at the age of eighty-three.

Bullock's Pigs Disrupted Diplomatic Relations

Alphonse de Saligny, the charge' d'affaires of King Louis Phillipe, had been with the French legation in Washington just before coming to Texas in 1839 to represent France, the first European nation to extend recognition to the Republic. Saligny was impressed by the potential of the new country but not by the rough frontier people.

Saligny bought land from Anson Jones in 1840 and started construction of the embassy. Saligny sold the house and lot to Bishop John Odin of San Antonio, with the privilege of occupying it for one year before giving possession to the bishop. The house was of frame construction on a rock foundation. The doors, windows, and hardware came from France.

The city of Houston was raw enough when Saligny arrived there, but Austin was even worse. Saligny wrote, "I have for a long time suffered . . . from the many hogs with which this town is infested. Every morning one of my domestics spends two hours in putting up and nailing the palings of the fence, which these animals threw down for the purpose of eating the corn of my horses; one hundred and forty pounds of nails have been used for this purpose. One day these hogs entered even to my chamber and ate my towels and destroyed my papers."

The pigs at issue belonged to Austin innkeeper Richard Bullock, to whom Saligny was still indebted for room and board prior to moving into the embassy. The pigs destroyed Saligny's garden, and he authorized his servant to kill some of them, which the servant did. The outraged Bullock attacked the — as a New Orleans newspaper put it — "unlucky murderer, bunging up his eyes and phlabotomizing his nose in a maneuver to appease the ghosts of the slaughtered innocents."

Saligny considered the honor of France sullied by Bullock and demanded severe punishment consistent with "the enormity of the offense," which was an "odious violation of the law of nations." Bullock's position was that Saligny should have maintained a better fence.

Bullock was arrested and released on bond, which Saligny felt was casual treatment. Saligny did not receive excessive sympathy from Austin officials because of his failure to pay debts and his passing of counterfeit promissory notes. A few days after the attack on the servant, the American minister wrote the Texas Secretary of State, "on the afternoon of yesterday, the Hon Alphonso De Saligny Charge' d'affaires of the King of France, whilst in the act of visiting my family, at my lodgings, and when within the enclosure of the yard, was rudely and violently assaulted by Mr. Richard Bullock of this City. . . ."

Bullock was again arrested and admitted to bail. The prosecution did not move fast enough for Saligny. He departed for Galveston, where he tried to stir up public opinion against the government.

The serious side of the incident was that Texas was then trying to borrow in France some 35,000,000 francs. Saligny's brother-in-law, the French Minister of Finance, after learning of the Bullock incident, opposed the loan, and it was not made.

The French Legation, at San Marcos and East Eighth in Austin, was built in 1840.

Houston Was Baptized at Independence Church

Cole's Settlement was begun in 1824. Its name was changed to Independence after the Declaration of Independence was signed at nearby Washington.

On August 31, 1839, the Reverend Thomas Spraggins met with half a dozen prospective members to organize the Independence Baptist Church, the ninth in Texas. Two years later the pastor reported, "The Church is small but the congregation is the largest in the Republic."

The church was meeting in the building of Independence Female Academy. When Baylor University was opened at Independence in 1845 the Academy structure was used for classrooms. Baylor's first president was also the pastor of Independence Church, Reverend Henry Graves. The Reverend George Washington Baines, of North Carolina, Lyndon Baines Johnson's great grandfather, was pastor from 1850 to 1852. He was also president of Baylor for two years. In 1851, Rufus Burleson became president of Baylor, and Horace Clark was made principal of the female department. Burleson was pastor of Independence Baptist Church from 1854 to 1856.

Sam Houston's wife and mother-in-law were members of Independence Church when Houston decided to join. After talking with Baines at length Houston was baptized by Burleson on November 19, 1854. The regular baptistry at Kounty Creek had been filled with limbs and debris by pranksters, so Houston's baptism was performed at Little Rocky Creek. Houston told the preacher, "Dr. Burleson, you have baptized my pocketbook," and Burleson said, "Thank God. I wish the pocketbook of every Baptist had been baptized."

A church periodical commented, "The announcements of General Houston's immersion has excited the wonder and surprise of many who have supposed that he was 'past praying for' but it is no marvel to us .... Three thousand and fifty clergymen have been praying for him since the Nebraska outrage in the Senate."

A friend said, "Well General, I hear your sins were washed away," and Houston answered, ". . .Lord help the fish down below."

Mrs. Houston's mother, Nancy Lea, gave five hundred silver dollars to the church to buy a bell, which arrived in late 1856. When Mrs. Lea died she was buried "within the sound of the bell." Margaret Lea Houston's grave is beside hers. The 113 year-old bell dropped from its moorings in March, 1969, and broke into several pieces. It was restored and is on display at the church.

The present church was built in 1872 after the original adobe structure burned.

The present Independence Baptist Church, of Independence, Washington County, was built in 1872 after its predecessor burned.

John Neely Bryan Founded Dallas

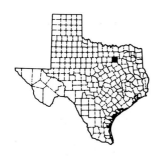

John Neely Bryan of Tennessee lived with the Cherokee four years and platted Van Buren, Arkansas, before coming to Texas. He was at Holland Coffee's trading post on the Red River when the Texas Congress ordered a road blazed from that place to Austin.

In the fall of 1841, at the Trinity crossing of the road connecting Coffee's place and Austin, Bryan settled near the present Dallas County courthouse. Shortly before Bryan's arrival some rangers brought their families to Bird's Fort, twenty-two miles north and west of the Bryan site. From that settlement, Mabel Gilbert and James Beeman moved to Bryan's neighborhood. Later the Gilberts moved to Fannin County, but Beeman's daughter, Margaret, age eighteen, married the thirty-three year old Bryan at Fort Inglish — present Bonham — which was the closest place with someone empowered to perform weddings.

The Indians in the area disappeared after the Battle of Village Creek, so that instead of establishing a trading post, as he had intended, Bryan decided to found a town. A site half a mile square was surveyed in 1844 by J. P. Dumas. Bryan was somewhat apprehensive about his legal position since the area was under contract to the Peters Colony proprietors.

Dallas County was created by the first legislature on March 30, 1846, when Dallas had about forty residents. Four years later a county seat election was held and Dallas got 191 votes; Hord's Ridge — at Marsalis Park in present Oak Cliff — polled 178, and Cedar Springs, three miles north, polled 101. A second election was required, and Dallas defeated Hord's Ridge 244 to 216.

Bryan joined the gold seekers in 1849; only one of Dallas' adult males failed to make the journey to the gold fields. Bryan returned, having met with no success. He spent considerable time drinking, and he sold the rest of his Dallas lots in 1852.

Three years later Bryan shot a drunk and fled, thinking he had killed him. The man recovered, but Bryan stayed away from Dallas almost six years. He lived in the Creek Nation for awhile and worked worn-out gold mines in California. In 1861 he finally came back to his family in Dallas. He spent about a year in Confederate service, but at fifty-one he did not have sufficient endurance and strength to soldier. Bryan moved out by White Rock Creek. His mind started to deteriorate and he was admitted to the mental hospital at Austin in early 1877. He died a few months thereafter.

The cabin of cedar logs Bryan built for his bride in 1843 still stands. John William Rogers wrote, "Coming upon this cabin in the heart of modern downtown Dallas is a dramatic and poignant reminder of how recent were Dallas' humble pioneer beginnings. In spite of the little structure's primitive simplicity, perhaps because of it, there is something almost awesome about seeing with your very eyes, standing in the open and almost on its original site, the very first cabin ever raised in this wilderness that was to give place to a modern metropolis. What other great city has so intimate and personal a souvenir of its very beginning."

John Neely Bryan's cabin was moved two or three times before being located in the Dallas Historical Plaza, near its original site.

Anson Jones Was the Republic's Last President

Born in Great Barrington, Massachusetts, in 1798, Anson Jones began the practice of medicine when he was twenty-two. After several business and professional failures he reached Texas in 1833.

Jones developed a good practice at Brazoria. In the summer of 1835, as troubles with Mexico mounted, he urged an independence declaration. At San Jacinto he was an army surgeon but insisted upon remaining an infantry private. After independence Jones was a member of Congress and then minister to the United States. About the time Lamar recalled him, Jones was elected to the Senate, where he became a major critic of Lamar's policies.

In 1841, Jones became President Sam Houston's Secretary of State. Jones succeeded Houston as president on December 9, 1844, at which time the main issue before Texans was whether to become part of the United States. In the 1844 election James K. Polk, of Tennessee, favoring annexation, defeated Henry Clay. The retiring president, John Tyler, wanted Texas brought into the Union during his term, so the United States Senate and House resolved that Texas be annexed. In the meantime the British had persuaded Mexico to offer a treaty recognizing Texas independence if she would not join the United States.

To the Texas Congress, and a convention called for that purpose, Jones submitted the questions of annexation and the Mexican treaty. Both chose joinder to the United States. After adoption of the constitution drawn by the convention, the United States Congress, by approving that document, effected the admission of Texas on December 29, 1845.

The first state legislature met at Austin February 19, 1846. After both houses were organized they came together to witness the close of the Republic. President Anson Jones said, "The lone star of Texas, which ten years since arose amid clouds over fields of carnage, and obscurely seen for a while, has culminated . . . . The final act in the drama is now performed. The Republic of Texas is no more." As he lowered the flag of the Republic, the pole from which it had flown broke in two.

Andrew Jackson, who had hoped so long for Texas annexation, wrote, "I now behold the great American eagle, with her stars and stripes, hovering over the lone star of Texas. . . ."

After Jones turned over the government to Governor Henderson he retired to his plantation, Barrington, near Washington-on-the-Brazos. He did well financially in the next decade but he felt that he had not received the honors due him. He came to hate Sam Houston and thought he would be Houston's successor in the United States Senate. Then T. J. Rusk died, meaning the legislature would fill both seats in 1857; but Jones did not get a single vote, as J. Pinckney Henderson and John Hemphill were elected. On January 9, 1858, at Houston — in the hotel that had once been the capitol of the Republic — he killed himself.

Barrington, the home of Anson Jones, was moved to the state park at Washington-on-the-Brazos.

French Utopians Settled La Reunion

Francois Fourier believed that society should be structured in units of 1600 people. Each group would live together and cultivate its land in common. Victor Considerant, a Fourier disciple, came to the United States to make arrangements for a colony. A total of some 2,000 acres was selected across the Trinity from Dallas. In 1854 Considerant wrote a book, *Au Texas*, which praised the new land, and believers in Fourier's teachings came from France, Belgium, and Switzerland.

The first contingent came by water to Houston and walked from there, a twenty-six day ordeal. They arrived at Dallas in April, 1855, crossed the Trinity, and started building houses and cultivating their land. Their first crops were bad because of grasshoppers and drought, but their successful Fourth of July celebration was attended by many Dallas citizens.

At the colony, La Reunion, there were no schools; the children had work to do. Government was by a president and assembly. There was no church. Burials were not religious ceremonies. But the colonists did not follow Fourier's teachings on the abolition of marriage. Dallas justices of the peace and ministers performed their weddings.

Each family was assigned certain tasks. The community had a laundry, blacksmith shop, communal dining room, and a cooperative store. Colonists' houses were built on lots of uniform size.

One of La Reunion's problems was that it was an agricultural colony and only two colonists were farmers. The land that had been chosen was not the best, but probably the ultimate threat to the colony was the desire of the individual to profit from his own ability. The Swiss withdrew and moved across the Trinity, and as the more capable men kept leaving, La Reunion's collapse became only a matter of time. By 1858 the colony had had a total of some 350 members.

La Reunion dissolved. About 160 colonists moved to Dallas. Some went to New Orleans. Considerant and others returned to France. The former colonists contributed much to Dallas, where they were the first artists, scientists, and skilled artisans. For the very reasons that they could not succeed in farming they could make substantial contributions to the Dallas community.

One La Reunion colonist was Julien Reverchon. After the colony collapsed he farmed and began a botanical collection which included 20,000 specimens of more than 2,600 species. Eventually the collection was acquired by the Missouri Botanical Gardens at St. Louis. Several plants were named in his honor, such as the genus Reverchonia. He was professor of botany in the Baylor University College of Medicine for a decade before his death in 1905.

A golf course, stores, apartments, and a hospital occupy the French La Reunion colony tract in the Stevens Park area of Dallas' Oak Cliff.

The Mier Prisoners Were Buried at La Grange

In September, 1842, Mexican General Adrian Woll captured San Antonio. At La Grange, Nicholas Mosby Dawson, a San Jacinto veteran, raised a company to join a force Mathew Caldwell was taking from Gonzales to repulse the Mexicans.

On September 18, as Dawson and his fifty-three men were marching toward the Battle of the Salado, they encountered Mexican troops. Badly outnumbered, a mile and a half from the battleground, Dawson's men took shelter in a grove of mesquites. The Mexicans began firing artillery into the mesquite, killing a number of Texans. Dawson surrendered, but the Mexicans started firing again after some of the Texans had laid down their arms. Dawson and thirty-five others were killed. Three escaped and fifteen were taken prisoner.

Because of the Mexican invasions Alexander Somervell led an army to the Rio Grande. On December 19, 1842, Somervell, after having taken Laredo and Guerrero, ordered a return home, but some of his men decided to invade Mexico.

Thus was begun the Mier Expedition under William S. Fisher, whose men invaded Mier on Christmas. The battle lasted well into the next day, when the Texans surrendered. As some of the prisoners were marched to Mexico City an escape was attempted. Santa Anna ordered the 176 recaptured Texans executed. After Governor Francisco Mexia refused to obey, the order was amended to provide for the execution of every tenth man. Seventeen men drew black beans and were shot. Later Ewen Cameron was also executed since he had led the escape.

During the Mexican War Major Walter P. Lane took his men to Haciendo Salado, where the Mier men were buried; one of his soldiers, John E. Dusenberry, had drawn a white bean. The Haciendo Salado alcalde was forced to have the remains exhumed and placed in four large boxes. The boxes accompanied the army until the war ended, when Dusenberry took them to La Grange, which was the home of the highest ranking of the executed men, Captain William Mosby Eastland.

The boxes were stored in the courthouse temporarily. Then the bodies of the Dawson men were brought to La Grange. On the sixth anniversary of the Dawson Massacre, September 18, 1848, John Dusenberry was the main speaker as Sam Houston and others gathered for a military funeral and the burial of the Mier and Dawson men on a bluff overlooking the Colorado.

The original vault fell into disrepair, and in 1933 arrangements were made to enclose it within a new one of granite. During the centennial observance a forty-eight foot memorial shaft was erected.

The Mier prisoners and the victims of the Dawson Massacre were buried at Monument Hill, near La Grange, Fayette County, one of the most beautiful places in Texas.

Houston's Defense Counsel Was Francis Scott Key

Sam Houston held a great number and variety of substantial offices. Born in Virginia, he became a Tennessee district attorney, major general of militia, congressman, and governor. He was commanding general of the Texas Army, congressman and president of the Republic, United States Senator, and governor of the state of Texas.

In no position that he ever occupied was Houston accustomed to walking on tip-toe. He was acquainted with many kinds of trouble. After resigning as Tennessee's governor he returned to the Cherokee. He had lived with them in his youth. In 1832, while Houston was a member of an Indian delegation to Washington, Ohio Congressman William Stanberry, on the floor of the House, said some slanderous things about him. Houston sent a note preliminary to challenging Stanberry to a duel. Stanberry refused to answer but strapped on pistols.

Almost two weeks after the original insult Houston was going to his hotel one evening when he encountered Stanberry on Pennsylvania Avenue. Houston attacked the Ohio Congressman with his hickory cane. Stanberry drew one pistol, aimed, and pulled the trigger, but it did not fire.

Stanberry filed a complaint with the Speaker. The House voted to arrest Houston, since the offensive statement had been made in that chamber, and Congressmen were to be immune from accountability for statements made there. Houston's only punishment could be reprimand and withdrawal of his privilege, as a former Congressman, of coming onto the floor of the House.

Houston appeared the next day and was given forty-eight hours to prepare his defense. He retained attorney Francis Scott Key.

The trial began April 19. Stanberry showed the bumps on his head and Houston's cane was put into evidence. Key's defense was that the words which so inflamed Houston were not those spoken in the House — he did not hear those — but were those printed in a newspaper. It was a rather unsatisfactory position, since the newspaper account was a direct quote of Stanberry's speech in the House.

The trial lasted for a month and attracted a great deal of attention. President Jackson was displeased by the actions of his young friend, Houston, but said a few such chastisements would teach congressmen to maintain civil tongues.

The House found Houston guilty, but the attempt to deprive him of the privileges of the House was defeated by James K. Polk and other Jacksonians.

In the District of Columbia courts Houston was charged with the crime of assault, and a fine of $500 was imposed. A year later Houston asked about his unpaid fine and was advised, "Get that remitted by the Old Chief." After another year Houston wrote Andrew Jackson about the fine. By virtue of his pardoning power, the president granted a remission.

Sam Houston thought the upstairs porch of Woodland, his Huntsville home, was fine for afternoon naps.

Sam Houston Believed in the Union

After Lincoln's election, secession sentiment built in Texas until it was irresistible. In spite of his Unionist views Sam Houston had become governor in 1859. "Let us wait and see," he answered in response to demands that the legislature be convened to consider secession.

On December 20, 1860, South Carolina left the Union. Mississippi, Alabama, Georgia, and Louisiana followed, while Houston resisted the mounting pressures. In the meantime Oran M. Roberts and others issued a call for a convention to consider disunion. The Secession Convention met in Austin on January 28, 1861 and adjourned February 4, leaving a Committee of Public Safety to act for it. A resolution was adopted repealing the annexation ordinance of 1845 by a vote of 166 to 8. The resolution was to be submitted to a vote of the people on February 23, and if passed the secession was to be effective March 2, the anniversary of Texas independence and Sam Houston's birthday.

Houston took to the stump to urge hostile crowds to vote for union. At Galveston he told a mob, "Some of you laugh to scorn the idea of bloodshed as the result of secession. But let me tell you what is coming .... Your fathers and husbands, your sons and brothers, will be herded at the point of the bayonet .... You may, after the sacrifice of countless millions of treasure and hundreds of thousands of lives, as a bare possibility, win Southern independence .... but I doubt it. I tell you that while I believe with you in the doctrine of state rights, the North is determined to preserve this Union. They are not a fiery, impulsive people, as you are, for they live in colder climates. But when they begin to move in a given direction ... they move with the steady momentum and perseverance of a mighty avalanche; and what I fear is, they will overwhelm the South."

Texans voted 46,129 to 14,697 for disunion, and the Convention met again on March 2 to canvas the returns. Houston tried to keep Texas out of the Confederacy, knowing he would lose that battle also. The Secession Convention united Texas with the Confederate States on March 5. After Houston refused to swear allegiance to the Confederacy, the office of governor was declared vacant. Lieutenant Governor Edward Clark succeeded Houston.

The Reverend William Baker wrote in 1880: "As I look back into the darkness of those days, the central figure is that of the old governor (Houston) sitting in his chair in the basement of the capitol ... sorrowfully meditating what it were best to do .... The officer of the gathering upstairs summoned the old man three times to come forward and take the oath of allegiance ... to the Confederacy. I remember as yesterday the call thrice repeated — 'Sam Houston! Sam Houston! Sam Houston!' but the man sat silent, immovable, in his chair below, whittling steadily on."

Lincoln had offered assistance, but Houston, rather than cause fighting in Texas, stepped aside. His oldest son, eighteen year old Sam Jr., joined the Confederate Army and was taken prisoner at Shiloh.

In April, 1863, seventy-year old Sam Houston made his will. He died July 26 in a downstairs room of the Steamboat House in Huntsville.

146

Houston died in a downstairs room of the Steamboat House, near the campus of Sam Houston State University at Huntsville.

Sam Houston's grave is across the street from Huntsville High School.

Texans believed in Sam Houston, but they believed more strongly in secession.

General Twiggs Surrendered at the Main Plaza

David E. Twiggs, born in Georgia in 1790, was a captain in the War of 1812. He made colonel in the year of Texas independence. During the Mexican War he served with Zachary Taylor and was promoted to major general. He became commander of the Department of Texas in 1857.

As the nation threatened to dissolve over Lincoln's election, General Twiggs kept asking for instructions on the disposition of soldiers, forts, ammunition, guns, and other federal property if Texas were to secede. No orders were forthcoming. Next to General Winfield Scott, Twiggs, seventy years old, was the senior officer of the United States Army.

In January, 1861, Governor Houston asked Twiggs whether he would try to hold onto government property or turn it over to a state officer when secession came. Houston wrote, "This course is suggested by the fact . . . that an effort will be made by an unauthorized mob to take forcibly and appropriate the public stores. . . ." Houston wanted to minimize strife between the Army and the Texans when disunion came.

From San Antonio Twiggs replied, "I am without instructions from Washington in regard to the public property here, or the troops, in the event of the State's seceding. . . ." He sent Houston's letter to his superiors with his sixth request for orders. General Twiggs wrote, "As I do not think anyone in authority desires me to carry on a civil war against Texas, I shall, after secession, if the governor repeats his demand, direct the arms and other property to be turned over to his agents . . . . The troops in this department occupy a line of some twelve hundred miles, and some time will be required to remove them to any place. I again ask, what disposition is to be made of them?"

Several days before the secession election Ben McCulloch, acting for the Committee of Public Safety, demanded the arsenal and barracks at San Antonio. Twiggs complied on February 18, 1861, at Main Plaza, surrendering $3 million worth of federal property, including wagons, horses and mules, supplies, and a chain of forts. Because of Twiggs' surrender, the Army summarily dismissed him.

When Georgia seceded General Twiggs resigned his commission and became a Confederate major general. He saw very little service before he became physically unable to remain on active duty. He died July 15, 1862.

After the Mexican War General Twiggs had been given ceremonial swords by the United States, the Georgia legislature, and the city of Augusta. The swords were heavily ornamented and quite valuable. The handle of the one presented by the United States was set with jewels, and the scabbard was of solid gold. General Benjamin F. Butler, when he occupied New Orleans, took the swords into his possession. They were on display at the Treasury Department until General Twiggs' heirs finally recovered them in 1889.

For two and a half centuries history has been made at Main Plaza in San Antonio.

Forty-Two Men Died in Gainesville's Great Hangings

Cooke County was part of the Peters Colony, which sought settlers from the midwest as well as the south. By 1860 the population was 3760, about half from free states. The diverse origins of the Cooke Countians would contribute to the violence of 1862. In the secession election Cooke voted for the Union. Statewide, Texans ratified the ordinance of secession.

After Texas seceded, in March, 1861, tensions continued to mount in Cooke County. The Unionists resented having been taken into the Confederacy in spite of carrying their county. Many refused to join the army or permit their sons to do so. Southerners worried about their own lack of numbers. They had not been sufficiently numerous to win the election, and many of them were away in the army.

Then war news began reaching North Texas days before it appeared in newspapers, raising suspicions that Unionists were in touch with Northern troops. If there were such contacts, an attack on the Confederates might be possible.

Southern suspicions seemed to be confirmed in late 1862 when a drunk offered to initiate the mailman into an organization which planned to kill the southerners and take North Texas into the Union.

A spy sent to join the so-called Peace Party reported that it had a large number of members and that an attack was planned. Arrests began October 1. For thirteen days bands of armed men combed the countryside. Between 150 and 250 men were arrested and brought into Gainesville. Many had had no dealings with the Peace Party. Numerous grudges were being settled.

A mob which had taken charge of affairs chose a twelve man jury to try complaints against the prisoners. The mob had grown to about four hundred armed men. After convicting seven prisoners the jurymen began having second thoughts. There was no provision in the law for such a tribunal, and they were sentencing men to hang. A rule was adopted requiring a two-thirds vote for conviction, which halted the hangings.

The jury decided to adjourn for a week so that passions might cool and the others could be freed. When the mob — which had broken into jail and hanged an army deserter — learned of the plan it sent spokesmen who chose fourteen men from a list; they were hanged on October 12 and 13, bringing the total to twenty-one. Two had been shot trying to escape.

It appeared that the trouble was over, but on October 16 Jim Dickson was ambushed while deer hunting. Colonel William Young — after whom Young County was later named — was killed while pursuing Dickson's murderers. The mob was furious. When the jury convened on the 18th it convicted nineteen men. They were hanged the following Sunday.

All forty executions took place on the limb of a great elm tree. A member of the jury wrote, "...the men would be hauled down California Street to that old historic tree, which is now dead and lies as still where it has been hauled as the bodies of the men who were hung on its long limbs lie in the grave."

Pecan Creek flows across the site of Gainesville's great elm tree where, in **1862**, forty men were hanged by their friends and neighbors.

The Chisholm Trail Was a Beef Highway

There was some trailing of beeves from Texas before 1861, but pre-Civil War activity was slight when compared to the hundreds of herds driven north after Appomattox.

When peace came, some five million longhorns were grazing the southern part of Texas. They were the descendants of Spanish cattle which had, through a century and a half of running free, developed extensive horns and great stamina. Bulls fought to the death over cows, producing a ratio of one bull to 30 cows; only the toughest of the bulls propagated. They were usually the ones with the longest horns. Typically, wild Texas cattle had horns measuring from 42 inches to six feet, although some exceeded eight feet.

Men coming home from the war found that cattle cost $4 to $5 a head in Texas, but in the North and East they sold for $40 to $50. The problem was getting the product to market. Trailing was hazardous because of the hostility of farmers and the laws of several states prohibiting Texas cattle. Herds of longhorns carried the Texas fever; they were immune but other cattle were not. Wherever Texas stock went, domestic animals died of the fever.

In 1866 a number of herds were taken north, the drovers not knowing where they would find buyers. Some found no market. Others were chased back into the Indian Territory by angry Kansas and Missouri farmers. What was needed was a point toward which drives might be directed with safety and assurance that the cattle would be bought.

Before the war the drives to the midwest had been up the Shawnee Trail, which crossed the eastern part of the Indian Territory and ended at St. Louis, Sedalia, Kansas City, and St. Joseph. But that country was practically closed.

Joseph McCoy of Springfield, Illinois, a cattle dealer, attacked the problem. He chose a shipping point within the Kansas quarantine, yet so far west that no one would try to enforce the law. McCoy made arrangements with the Union Pacific railroad whereby he would be paid about $5 a carload for cattle shipped from his stockyards.

Six-year old Abilene was the location McCoy chose. It consisted of a dozen or so rough log buildings. McCoy built a hotel and stockyard and sent out handbills telling of the new facilities. Drovers in the Indian Territory without specific destinations changed course for Abilene. The first shipment of cattle went out by railroad on September 5, 1867, before McCoy's hotel and stockyard were completed.

The news was welcomed in Texas. A new route, some 150 miles west of the Shawnee Trail, was opened across the Indian Territory. About 220 miles of the new course lay along a trail that had been used by trader Jesse Chisholm between modern Wichita, Kansas and Council Grove, near present Oklahoma City.

Chisholm, born in Tennessee, part Scot and part Cherokee, had lived in the Indian Territory for many years. Well respected by Indians and whites, and fluent in fourteen Indian languages, he had served as a guide and interpreter on many occasions. Jesse Chisholm died in early 1868 just before the heavy trailing began.

Within a short time Chisholm's name was applied to the entire network of trails

A bridge spans the Brazos at a Hill County crossing used by drovers taking herds up the Chisholm Trail.

leading from South Texas to Kansas. The Chisholm Trail began at the tip of Texas and was identical to the Shawnee Trail below Waco. The Shawnee passed Dallas, crossed the Red River at Preston, and left the Indian Territory at its northeast corner, but from Waco the Chisholm Trail passed Fort Worth and Decatur, entered the Indian Territory at Red River Station, and headed almost due north.

McCoy shipped almost a thousand cattle cars in 1867. One hundred fifty thousand head were driven to Abilene the next year. By 1870, when even the most stubborn cattlemen had accepted McCoy's idea, Abilene-bound herds totaled 300,000 longhorns. The peak year was 1871, when 700,000 head went up the trail. Abilene citizens had elected Joseph McCoy their mayor. Meanwhile Ellsworth and other places farther west were coveting Abilene's good fortune.

In time the country built up and the drives were fenced out, causing the herds to move westward. The railroads had reached Texas, but for a few years it remained more profitable to trail north than to pay the high freight rates. Dodge City became the main cattle market and the Western Trail superseded the Chisholm route.

The Chisholm Trail caused many changes in the country. It enabled cattlemen to bring large sums of money into Texas, which had always been short on capital. By providing a route to a precise destination some standardization was possible and trailing became more businesslike. The trail stimulated the settlement of the West, caused Chicago and Kansas City to develop, and made railroads expand and improve facilities for refrigerating cargo. And finally, the Chisholm Trail provided material for several generations of tellers of tales and lovers of the wild and open and free and easy.

—*The Cattleman*

Jesse Chisholm, part Cherokee, was a trader in the Indian Territory.

Sam Bass Intended to Rob the Round Rock Bank

Sam Bass — who "was born in Indiana. It was his native state" — was orphaned at twelve and came to Texas when he was nineteen.

After awhile as a cowhand he bought a race horse. Jenny, the Denton Mare, won with regularity and brought in as much as $500 a race. Charley Tucker, Bass' Negro jockey, rode bareback with only a trace of molasses on the mare's sides to help him keep his seat.

After a couple of years Bass sold Jenny and drove a herd up the Chisholm Trail. At Deadwood, he gambled away the proceeds from the cattle drive. To recoup he and his friends, with Joel Collins their leader, started holding up stagecoaches. In September, 1877, they took more than $60,000 in a Nebraska train robbery.

After Collins and two others were killed, Bass returned to Denton County. He began plundering stagecoaches, then robbed four trains within twenty miles of Dallas. Texas had never seen anything like it.

The railroad jobs had not yielded much, so Bass, looking for a bank to rob, decided on one at Round Rock, Williamson County. He, Jim Murphy, Seaborn Barnes, and Frank Jackson, reached Round Rock July 14, 1878. Their horses needed rest, so Bass planned to rob the bank on July 20, a Saturday.

Jim Murphy had already informed the rangers. Major John B. Jones took some of his men to Round Rock. Bass had seen the lawmen and suspected their identities. He and Jackson and Barnes went into town on Friday afternoon to look for rangers. Murphy remained behind.

Jones had told Williamson County Deputy Sheriff A.W. Grimes about Bass' plans. Grimes and Maurice B. Moore, a Travis County deputy, followed Bass and his companions into Henry Koppel's store. When Grimes asked Bass if he had a pistol, the three outlaws opened fire. Grimes was killed instantly. The firing continued as Bass and the others left the store. Moore was wounded in the chest; Sam Bass had lost two fingers on his right hand.

Rangers and citizens joined the chase as the outlaws ran for their horses. Bass was shot in the back. Barnes was killed. Jackson helped Bass up, and the two rode away. They took cover three miles from town in a live oak thicket. Bass insisted that Jackson leave. The next morning rangers found Bass near a work gang of railroad section hands. He was taken into Round Rock where he died on Sunday, July 21, his 27th birthday.

Frank Jackson was indicted for murder but was never tried. As late as 1927 people claiming to represent him attempted, unsuccessfully, to get his indictment dismissed. Jackson was rumored to have lived out his days as a substantial and respected New Mexico rancher.

After racing horses and holding up stagecoaches and trains, Sam Bass was killed while planning a Round Rock bank robbery.

Captain King Died at the Menger Hotel

William Menger's hotel, opened in February, 1859 on the Alamo Plaza near his brewery, was the best tavern in nineteenth century Texas. After the Civil War it was unofficial headquarters for the cattle business.

Among the Menger's guests were generals Robert E. Lee and Philip Sheridan, Secretary of War William Belknap, and presidents Ulysses S. Grant and Theodore Roosevelt. The poet Sidney Lanier stayed there, and O. Henry, William Sydney Porter, used the Menger in his stories.

Gas lights were installed in 1879 and the hotel was enlarged. In 1887 the Menger opened a bar that was a replica of the taproom in the English House of Lords. The hotel made its own beer and chilled it in the waters of the Alamo Madre ditch, which ran through the courtyard.

A Harper's Magazine writer said of her visit in 1877, "As you alight at the Menger, enter a narrow, unevenly-stoned passage, and come out upon a broad flagged courtyard surrounded on three sides by open galleries, with the stars overhead, and the lamplight flaring on a big mulberry tree growing in it below, you feel that you are in the heart of old Spain."

When Captain Richard King could no longer ignore his stomach cancer he came from the Rancho Santa Gertrudis to the Menger to die. There were few hospitals then, and those who were ill and away from home were treated in hotels. Captain King was attended by Dr. Ferdinand Herff, one of Texas' greatest physicians.

Friends and family came to pay their respects to Richard King once more. He made his will on April 2, 1885 and died a dozen days later. He had transformed a huge and empty and harsh country into the great King Ranch. Funeral services were held at the Menger, and Captain King was buried at San Antonio. Later his body was moved to Kingsville.

Once when Captain King and his family were staying at the Menger, Mrs. King had asked that water be sent to their room, which faced onto the balcony. After awhile Captain King became impatient. He took the big white pitcher out to the edge of the balcony and threw it down into the lobby. Pieces of the broken pitcher scattered all over the marble floor, and the noise startled everyone. When the room clerk looked up, King shouted, "If we can't get any water up here, we don't need a pitcher."

San Antonio's Menger Hotel was headquarters for cowmen, soldiers, and celebrities.

Ike Thought He Was Born in Tyler

David Dwight Eisenhower — he later reversed the order of his names — was born October 14, 1890, at Denison, Texas. His father worked in the Katy railroad shops. David and Ida Stover Eisenhower lived in Denison less than two years and returned to Kansas when the future president was only a few months old. The rest of their children were born in Dickinson County, Kansas.

Thus, a Kansas family had spent a few months in Texas, and, having made no impression upon the community, had moved away. For half a century no one took particular notice of the child who had been born in Denison. During World War II, Dwight Eisenhower, an obscure lieutenant colonel only a few years before, became commander of the Normandy invasion.

At Denison Miss Jeanie Jackson was a member of the 21 Club, a women's group. She was an elderly retired teacher. Many of the other members had been her students. At a meeting of the 21 Club someone mentioned the birthday of General Eisenhower. Miss Jackson said she knew some people named Eisenhower who had lived at the corner of Day and Lamar streets a long time ago. A baby had been born there, she said. She had rocked that baby, and she thought that baby had to be General Eisenhower.

Someone said Eisenhower was from Kansas. Someone else suggested that if Miss Jeanie believed she was correct she should write to the general. The club turned to other matters.

Dwight Eisenhower answered Miss Jeanie's inquiry. She was mistaken, he said. He was born in Texas. That much was true. But it was his understanding that he was born in Tyler.

There was one way to be sure, General Eisenhower said; if Miss Jeanie cared to ask his mother he was certain she would be happy to respond.

Miss Jeanie Jackson wrote to Mrs. David Eisenhower in Abilene, Kansas; she replied promptly. Indeed her son was born in Denison, she said. Dwight was her third child. While they lived on Lamar Street a Mr. Redmond boarded with them, and she remembered that Jeanie Jackson lived in a rented room across the railroad tracks.

Miss Jeanie reported her findings to the club and was commended. Soon afterward efforts were commenced to acquire and restore the house on Lamar Street. When General Eisenhower came to Denison in 1946, Miss Jeanie rode with him in the welcoming parade. And Earl Eisenhower visited her in the hospital in 1956, not long before her death.

On all of Eisenhower's military records but one, Tyler was shown as his birthplace. The exception was his West Point application. Evidently he had gotten it into his mind that he was born in Tyler. When he applied for the military academy he consulted his mother, filled in Denison on the form, forgot, and went back to believing Tyler was his birthplace.

After he left the presidency, General Eisenhower wrote of his father's coming to Texas: "In 1883, only three years after his marriage, he had found his business gone, his family growing, and he was without a job and in debt. When drought and grasshoppers

162

David Eisenhower, a wiper for the Missouri, Kansas, and Texas Railroad, rented a house at Lamar and Day in Denison. His son, Dwight, was born in the front room on the right.

struck simultaneously, and southern Dickinson County, Kansas, a wholly agricultural community, was in distress, Father had such good relations with his suppliers that he and his partner were able to continue extending credit to their customers. Naturally, he and Mother were living on almost nothing but it had appeared that they would pull through. It was just at that moment that his partner decided to disappear, taking whatever small assets there were remaining, and leaving my dad holding the sack.

"In after years, he could not be brought to talk about the experience. But, as I noted, he had started all over again, at the bottom, in the M K & T (Katy) shops at Denison . . . ."

"His temper could blaze with frightening suddenness but when things were going along at a casual tempo, he was a good companion . . . His finest monument was his reputation in Abilene and Dickinson County . . . Because of it, all central Kansas helped me secure an appointment to West Point in 1911, and thirty years later, it did the same for my son John. I'm proud he was my father. My only regret is that it was always so difficult to let him know the great depth of my affection for him."

Eisenhower, called Ike by most Americans, accepted the surrender of Germany at the close of World War II; he was a five star general, president of Columbia University, commander of NATO forces, and thirty-fourth president of the United States. Late in life when he was asked if there was anything else he wished he could be, his answer was, "I wish I could be my grandson, David."

The family of David and Ida Stover Eisenhower sat for a photograph in Abilene, Kansas, in 1902. Dwight stood just behind his father's right shoulder.

O. Henry Was an Austin Bank Teller

William Sydney Porter, who, using the pen name O. Henry, became one of the most widely read of American writers — Russia issued a special postage stamp in 1962 to mark the centenary of his birth — came to Texas in 1882. He was a La Salle County ranch hand, an Austin pharmacist, and a real estate man. At the time of his marriage, in 1887, he was a draftsman at the Land Office, earning $100 a month.

Porter worked for Austin's First National Bank from 1891 until 1894. He quit the bank to devote his full time to the *Rolling Stone*, a humorous weekly he published for awhile. In July, 1896, while working for the *Houston Post,* Porter was arrested and charged with embezzling $845 from the Austin bank. He fled to Honduras.

Learning of his wife's illness, Porter returned to Austin in 1897. He was convicted of embezzlement and sentenced to the penitentiary. Porter sold his first story just before going to prison; he wrote several while there which were published under various pseudonyms, including O. Henry.

After serving three years and ninety days, Porter went to New York. He was a prolific writer, producing 115 stories in a single two-year period. Many of his stories were set in Austin; he described San Antonio's bridges and the Menger Hotel bar, so that later the hotel advertised, "Teddy Roosevelt recruited his Rough Riders in the Menger Bar. Here, too, O. Henry dreamed and wrote many of his world renowned stories."

Porter's fiction has been published in forty languages. He remarried in 1907, died June 5, 1910 in New York, and was buried in his native state, North Carolina.

From 1893 to 1895, William Sydney Porter lived in an Austin house now maintained by the city as the O. Henry Museum.

Lieutenant Foulois Was the American Air Force

Although several other nations wanted to use their invention, Wilbur and Orville Wright believed the United States should have first priority. The Army, disinterested, finally was pressured into establishing an Aeronautical Division in the Signal Corps to investigate the military uses of heavier-than-air machines. In December, 1907, the army called for bids on an air vehicle.

The Wrights submitted the best bid. In September, 1908, at Fort Myer, Virginia, as Orville Wright and Lieutenant Thomas E. Selfridge tested the contract airplane, it crashed. Selfridge was killed and Wright was hospitalized for seven months. With another machine, on June 27, 1909, Orville Wright and Lieutenant Frank P. Lahm stayed aloft seventy-two minutes at 42.6 miles per hour. On July 30, Orville Wright and his passenger, Lieutenant Benjamin D. Foulois, flew from Fort Myer to Alexandria, Virginia, and back, a ten mile trip before some 7,000 spectators. The airplane was accepted.

The contract required the Wrights to teach two men to fly. Lieutenant Lahm and Lieutenant Frederic E. Humphreys soloed October 26 at College Park, Maryland and were then ordered back to the Cavalry and Engineers. Foulois became the only Aeronautical Division officer. Later Major General Foulois wrote, ". . .I was not entirely unqualified. I had logged fifty-four minutes of passenger time with Wilbur Wright . . . . But I had never been up in the machine alone, taken it off, or landed it."

Foulois and the airplane were sent to Fort Sam Houston in February, 1910. Foulois, a balloonist, was ordered to "take plenty of spare parts and teach yourself to fly." He and his nine enlisted men uncrated and assembled the airplane, using wire, twine, and stovebolts. Passersby called, "Whatcha making boys, a kite?"

Foulois wrote of the test flight at 9:30 a.m. on March 2, "Eight men delicately lifted Aeroplane No. 1 and Army Aviator No. 1 to the launching track . . . . I couldn't discern it above the noise of my engine, but reporters said 'a reverent hush fell over the crowd.' This was appropriate, for I was praying." Foulois got the plane off the ground, to a height of a hundred feet, remained aloft for 7½ minutes at fifty miles an hour, and set it down safely on the parade ground.

Because the budget for the airplane's operation was only $150 — and even though he was paying some expenses out of his own pocket — Foulois was able to fly only nine hours in the next seven months. He improved the airplane by adding landing wheels, but it was worn out by the end of the year. Foulois borrowed a plane from a civilian to carry out his unit's activities.

On March 3, 1911, he demonstrated the military use of the airplane by flying 106 miles from Laredo to Eagle Pass in two hours and ten minutes. Congress authorized the purchase of five airplanes.

The United States was no longer a one-plane power.

On San Antonio's Fort Sam Houston parade ground the sole officer in the United States air arm taught himself to fly the army's only aeroplane.

Battleship Texas Was at Iwo Jima

The first battleship *Texas* was a Confederate ironclad which was captured by the federals when Richmond fell in April, 1865. The second, the *USS Texas*, was built at the Norfolk Navy Yard in 1892. Her ship's complement was thirty officers and 478 enlisted men. She saw action in the Spanish-American War and brought back the bodies of those who died in the sinking of the *USS Maine*. In March, 1911, the obsolete *USS Texas* was sunk in Chesapeake Bay by other ships of the fleet.

A new *USS Texas*, authorized by Congress in 1910, was commissioned in March, 1914. Her length was 573 feet, approximately twice that of her 301 foot predecessor. The *Texas* was the ultimate in naval architecture. Capable of a speed of twenty-one knots, she was one of the finest gunnery ships in the world.

The *Texas* saw her first action on January 30, 1918, when she fired on a German submarine. She was part of President Wilson's escort to the peace talks, and in 1919 was the first American ship to carry aircraft. Modernized in 1925, she was the flagship of Admiral Ernest King, the Atlantic fleet commander, when Pearl Harbor was attacked. She saw action at Casa Blanca, Gibraltar, and Morocco.

On June 6, 1944, at 5:50 a.m. the *Texas'* batteries began clearing the way for the D Day invasion of Normandy. Her targets were at the western end of Omaha Beach. Troops began landing less than an hour later. Throughout the day she answered calls to fire on troops, batteries, and vehicles. One mission was the shelling of a tank concentration that was firing into American troops near Grandcamp.

It was necessary that the Allies capture Cherbourg, the nearest major port to the invaded area. Without that facility the ability of the Allies to supply their troops was subject to the capriciousness of the English Channel. On June 25, the *Texas* was shelling German coastal defenses at Cherbourg when her navigation bridge was destroyed. The helmsman was killed and eleven men were injured.

After repairs were made, the *Texas* took part in the Pacific campaign. For three days she shelled Japanese positions on Iwo Jima prior to the landing by Marines on February 19, 1945. For three weeks the *Texas* continued the bombardment, firing 923 rounds of 14 inch ammunition and 967 rounds of 5 inch. Her crew remained at battle stations for fifty days.

After the war, and past retirement age, the *Texas* was to be scrapped. She had spent 478 days in action against the enemy and had traveled 121,000 wartime miles. The Battleship Texas Commission was created by the legislature, and Texans gave some $80,000 to establish the thirty-four year old ship in Texas. The *Texas* became the first battleship named after a state to be retired to that state as a monument. She was moored at the San Jacinto battleground on April 21, 1948.

The *USS Texas*, after some **120,000 miles** of wartime action, is permanently berthed at the San Jacinto battleground.

The Grandcamp Exploded at Texas City

At 9:12 on the morning of April 16, 1947, the French freighter *Grandcamp* exploded five hundred yards from the Monsanto plant at Texas City, setting off fires and other explosions. Five hundred and seventy-six people were killed, 5,000 injured, and $67 million worth of property was destroyed.

The Texas City blast was the third major disaster in twenty-three days. An April 9 tornado in the Texas panhandle and Western Oklahoma had killed some 133, and a coal mine explosion took the lives of 111 miners in late March.

Texas City, the state's fourth ranking port, had a population of about 12,000. Its growth had been rapid during the war because of the location there of a plant to produce styrene for synthetic rubber. The plant had been built by the government and sold to the Monsanto Chemical Company after the war. It had about five hundred employees in 1947 and was only a short distance from the waterfront. There were hundreds of storage tanks containing oil, gasoline, and chemicals in the area.

On the morning of the explosion the crew noticed smoke coming from Number 4 hold on the *Grandcamp*, which was partially loaded with ammonium nitrate fertilizer. A crewman started spraying the cargo with a fire extinguisher. As the smoke increased he closed the hatch and turned on the steam in the compartment to smother the flames. The fire, probably caused by a cigarette, continued until it created enough pressure to blow the cover off the hatch.

An alarm had been turned in and a crowd had gathered. Firefighters seemed to have the fire under control when the *Grandcamp's* first explosion occurred. The Monsanto plant then exploded. Huge chunks of flaming metal showered Texas City, destroying homes and businesses and killing and injuring people. Nothing remained of the *Grandcamp*. Two airplanes were knocked out of the sky, killing four. The blasts were heard in Houston and caused damage in Galveston, sixteen miles away.

Dozens of fires were started, including one aboard the 7,000 ton freighter, *High Flyer*, which was loaded with 900 tons of ammonium nitrate. Firemen from four towns were pouring water on the *High Flyer*, with little effect. That freighter exploded an hour after midnight, at 1:10 a.m., April 17.

The *Grandcamp's* anchor, now situated in front of the Recreation Center, was blown through the air 1.62 miles; the huge chunk of steel — which weighed 3200 pounds originally — was buried ten feet in the ground.

The search for the missing began. Physicians came from Houston and other nearby cities. The city auditorium was turned into a hospital. A school gymnasium served as a morgue. Identification was made difficult or impossible because of the extent of injury to the victims. A Department of Public Safety team identified those whose fingerprints were on file. Eleven days after the explosion the identified dead numbered 433 and 302 people were still missing. Some have never been found.

Experts said that the early explosions were more powerful than the atom bombs dropped at Hiroshima and Nagasaki. Two hundred businesses and 3,382 homes were destroyed.

172

The Monsanto plant at Texas City, Galveston County, stands where the 1947 blast destroyed its predecessor.

John Kennedy Was Slain at the Triple Underpass

On January 20, 1961, the oldest man to serve as president, Dwight Eisenhower, was succeeded by the youngest man ever elected to that office. But John Kennedy's victory had been a narrow one. In 1960 he had polled 34,226,731 votes to Republican Richard Nixon's 34,108,157, a difference of a little over 1%. The electoral vote had been 303 to 219, but the change of a few thousand votes in Texas and Illinois would have made Richard Nixon president.

Because of his slim margin in Texas the president was quite concerned about the widening split in the Texas Democratic party. He wanted to be re-elected. A trip to Texas would contribute to party unity and might be the difference in keeping the state Democratic in 1964.

The President and Mrs. Kennedy left Washington on November 21, 1963. Enthusiastic crowds greeted them in San Antonio and Houston that afternoon. They arrived at Carswell Air Force Base about midnight and stayed at Fort Worth's Hotel Texas.

President Kennedy was to speak in the parking lot across from the hotel the next morning. It had been raining most of the night, but there was a good crowd waiting to hear him. The rain was still falling but had slackened as the president took his place behind the lectern that had been set up on the back of a flat bed truck. To those who had braved the bad weather he said, "There are no faint hearts in Fort Worth." The crowd cheered. Then someone shouted, "Where's Jackie?" The President said, "She is organizing herself. It takes her longer, but she looks better than we do when she does it."

At the Chamber of Commerce breakfast in the hotel the president mentioned that he had introduced himself in Paris as the man who accompanied Mrs. Kennedy there. "I am getting somewhat the same sensation as I travel around Texas," he said, "nobody cares about what Lyndon and I wear."

The President called John Nance Garner at Uvalde to wish him a happy birthday. Franklin Roosevelt's vice president was ninety-five years old. President Kennedy was to speak at Dallas' Market Hall at noon.

From Carswell, Air Force One got its altitude and began its glide to Dallas, a flight of a dozen minutes. At Love Field the President and Mrs. Kennedy shook hands with members of the crowd that had come to meet them and then got into the presidential limousine. Governor and Mrs. John Connally were sitting on the jump seats just in front of the President.

As they approached downtown Dallas the streets were thronged with people going to or coming from, lunch. Spectators crowded into the streets. The greetings were warm and enthusiastic.

At 12:29 p.m., as the President's limousine headed down Elm Street toward the triple underpass, bullets, fired from the Schoolbook Depository, struck President Kennedy and Governor Connally. At one p.m. the President was pronounced dead by physicians at Parkland Hospital.

From the right corner window of the Schoolbook Depository's sixth floor (just below the ledge), Lee Harvey Oswald assassinated John Fitzgerald Kennedy, President of the United States.

175

Oswald Was Captured at the Texas Theater

Immediately after the president was shot, policemen converged on the Schoolbook Depository. The building was sealed off. A witness had seen the killer and weapon in a sixth floor window.

An officer encountered Lee Harvey Oswald in the second floor lunchroom; the manager of the depository identified him as an employee. Oswald had come in off the street and asked for a job a little over a month before and had been hired to fill orders for books.

Oswald bought a Coca Cola from a machine and walked, unnoticed, out the front door. As the depository employees were checked, Oswald's absence was discovered. He then became the prime suspect.

At the sixth floor window, three cartridge shells were found. Boxes of books had been arranged as a sniper's perch. One box bore Oswald's palm print. Across the room a rifle was discovered partially hidden by book cartons. It proved to be the weapon that had killed the president. Oswald had bought it from a mail order firm.

At 12:40, ten minutes after the shooting, Oswald got on a bus that was stalled in traffic on Elm Street. He became impatient, got a transfer, and left the bus. Oswald then took a taxi from the Greyhound bus station to Beckley Street in Oak Cliff, a few blocks from where he had a room rented in the name of O.H. Lee. His landlady saw him rush into his room, put on a jacket, and leave.

On East Tenth Street, Police Officer J.D. Tippit stopped Oswald. Just after Tippit got out of the police car, Oswald shot him four times with a pistol and ran away. A witness used the radio in Tippit's car to report the shooting.

Police squads began searching the Jefferson Street area. Oswald was reported to be in the Oak Cliff Branch Library, but investigators found that the young man seen running into the library was only an excited employee rushing to tell his friends what had happened. Then a cashier at the Texas theater reported that a man had come in who acted strangely. The description he gave fit the one police were working on.

Officers entered the theater, which was almost deserted, from the front and back. Oswald was sitting near the rear of the auditorium. As Officer M.N. McDonald approached, Oswald said, "This is it. It's all over now." He hit McDonald, then tried to shoot him, but the pistol misfired. McDonald was still trying to take the gun when other officers came to his aid.

Oswald was taken to City Hall and questioned. Charges were filed against him about 7 p.m. for the murder of Officer Tippit. Oswald was charged with the assassination of President Kennedy later and was arraigned about 1:30 a.m. the next day.

On the morning of November 24, 1963, as Oswald was being transferred from City Hall to the county jail, Jack Ruby, the proprietor of a Dallas night club, shot and killed him.

After the assassination Lee Harvey Oswald fled to Oak Cliff, killed Dallas police officer J. D. Tippit, and fought policemen who arrested him in the Texas Theater on Jefferson Street.

177

A Presidential Library Was Built in Austin

The death of John Kennedy on November 22, 1963, brought to the presidency a Texan who, by experience, was eminently qualified for the office.

Born August 27, 1908, in Blanco County, Lyndon Johnson graduated from Johnson City High School in 1924, worked in California for awhile, then came home to a job on a road gang. In 1927 he enrolled at Southwest Texas State Teachers College. At San Marcos, Johnson worked as a janitor, edited the newspaper, debated, made good grades, taught school for a year at Cotulla, and graduated in 1930.

Johnson, a Houston school teacher, worked in Richard Mifflin Kleberg's congressional campaign in 1931 and then became Kleberg's secretary. In Washington, Congressman Sam Rayburn — who would later be Speaker of the House of Representatives longer than any other man — took an interest in him.

Johnson married Claudia Taylor, of Karnack, in 1934. In the following year he became head of the National Youth Administration in Texas. The purpose of the N.Y.A. was to get young people off the streets and into jobs and schools; Johnson, 27, was its youngest state administrator.

In 1937 Congressman James Buchanan died. Johnson filed to succeed him. Against nine opponents, most of them better known than he was, Johnson endorsed Franklin Roosevelt's plan to add justices to the Supreme Court when those of age failed to retire. Johnson's position made him the target of the other candidates and brought him the votes of all of the district's New Deal supporters. He received nearly twice as many ballots as the runner-up in the special election.

President Roosevelt was fishing in the Gulf soon after Lyndon Johnson's victory. The president's program had aroused much opposition; few congressmen were willing to run on a New Deal platform. Roosevelt asked to meet Johnson. From Galveston, Johnson rode through Texas on Roosevelt's special train.

After Senator Morris Sheppard died in April, 1941, Governor W. Lee O'Daniel appointed Andrew Jackson Houston, the son of Sam Houston, to fill the vacancy. After a few days in the Senate, Houston died. O'Daniel, Congressman Martin Dies, and Attorney General Gerald C. Mann were among the opponents Johnson faced in the special election. Over half a million ballots were cast and O'Daniel edged Johnson by 1,311 votes.

After Pearl Harbor, Johnson, a reserve lieutenant commander, had himself called to active duty in the Navy. In 1948 he announced for O'Daniel's Senate seat. Former Governor Coke Stevenson was his principal opponent. Stevenson drove an old car over the state, shaking hands. Johnson campaigned in a helicopter outfitted with a public address system. In the first primary Stevenson led Johnson, 477,077 to 405,617. The other nine candidates polled 320,000 votes, which made a runoff necessary.

Johnson won the second primary by only eighty-seven votes, 494,191 to Stevenson's 494,104. After lawsuits and threatened lawsuits Johnson was finally certified as the Democratic nominee. He defeated Jack Porter, of Houston, in the general election.

Johnson became Democratic Whip in early 1951; Vice President Alben Barkely said that he had earned "a reputation and a standing never exceeded in the same length of

The Lyndon Baines Johnson Library, on the campus of the University of Texas at Austin, houses some 31 million pages of the papers of the thirty-sixth president.

time by any other Senator." In the following year Senator Ernest McFarland of Arizona was defeated for re-election, and Johnson succeeded him as Senate Democratic leader. He was forty-four years old, the youngest man ever to lead either party in the Senate. He was the Democratic leader for eight years.

In 1960 Johnson tried for the Democratic presidential nomination, but John Kennedy's supporters were too well organized. With Johnson his running mate Kennedy barely defeated Richard Nixon. As vice president, Lyndon Johnson traveled 120,000 miles and represented the President in thirty-three countries.

After Johnson became president he demonstrated his ability to get legislation through the Senate and Congress; measures that had been advocated by John Kennedy became law. In 1964 the electorate showed its approval. He defeated Senator Barry Goldwater of Arizona by the greatest margin in history, receiving 61.2 per cent of the ballots cast.

But the tragedy of the war in Vietnam colored all else. In the midst of civil disorder and growing opposition, Lyndon Johnson announced that he would not seek re-election.

In 1965 the University of Texas suggested that the Johnson presidential library be located on its Austin campus. Each of the earlier libraries was in the president's home town: the Hoover Library at West Branch, Iowa; the Roosevelt Library at Hyde Park, New York; the Truman Library at Independence, Missouri; and the Eisenhower Library at Abilene, Kansas. The Johnson Library was the first to break that precedent and the first to be constructed on a University campus. Harvard will be the site of the John F. Kennedy Library.

The Lyndon Baines Johnson Library and School of Public Affairs was constructed by the University of Texas on a thirty-acre site at a cost of $18 million. It houses some 30 million pages of material dealing with Lyndon Johnson's thirty-one years in the House, Senate, Vice Presidency, and Presidency. At the May, 1971 dedication a barbecue was held for some 3,000 guests, including President Richard Nixon.

President Franklin Delano Roosevelt, fishing in the Gulf, got Governor James V. Allred to introduce him to young Lyndon Johnson, who had just won a congressional seat on a New Deal platform.

Glen Rose Got Sinclair's Dinosaurs

In 1930 an advertising man realized that Sinclair's motor oil came from petroleum that had been aging for a hundred million years before the advent of the dinosaur. To illustrate his point that the oldest crude oil was the best, he devised for Sinclair a campaign using dinosaurs.

It was the beginning of a forty year association between the Sinclair Oil Corporation and the dinosaur, particularly the seventy-foot, 40,000-pound *Brontosaurus.* That huge reptile — called the Thunder Lizard because the ground probably shook beneath his tread — came to symbolize Sinclair.

Advertisements in 104 newspapers and five national magazines used the dinosaur theme in the 1930 motor oil campaign. Public response was so good that dinosaur advertising was then utilized in selling all Sinclair products.

Experts, such as Dr. Barnum Brown of the American Museum of Natural History, were retained by Sinclair to assure authenticity. Sinclair began contributing funds to support the dinosaur-prospecting expeditions of Dr. Brown and others. *The Sinclair Dinosaur Book* was published in 1934 for use in schools.

In 1935 Sinclair gave away dinosaur albums and stamps. It was probably the company's most successful promotion. Children could pick up albums and stamps at Sinclair stations. In successive weeks stamps were issued portraying each of twelve kinds of dinosaurs. Four million albums were distributed and forty-eight million stamps bearing likenesses of giant reptiles from *Tyrannosaurus* to *Triceratops.*

At the New York World's Fair in 1964-5 some ten million visitors saw nine life-size fiberglass models of the mighty lizards that had ruled the earth 135 million years before. They were the creations of wildlife sculptor Louis Paul Jonas. Experts from Yale University and the American Museum of Natural History advised Jonas throughout their execution.

Jonas first made a small model of each dinosaur. Then a transparency was projected to actual size and traced on wallboards. Wire, cloth, burlap, and plaster were added to give shape. Modeling clay provided skin and facial detail. After being cut apart — and the brontosaur was broken into eighty-four pieces — fiberglass was applied. The completed fiberglass brontosaur, mounted on a steel frame, was sixty feet long, twenty feet high, and weighed 10,000 pounds.

After the World's Fair closed, the dinosaurs were exhibited at other events. Then in March, 1969, the Sinclair Oil Corporation was merged into the Atlantic Richfield Company. ARCO had already been chosen as Atlantic Richfield's new trade name; after the merger the Sinclair name and the dinosaur image were abandoned.

Sinclair's brontosaur and a Tyrannosaurus rex were donated to the Dinosaur State Park, which had been authorized that same year. Roland T. Bird, of the last generation of great dinosaur hunters, was present at Glen Rose in early 1970 as the new park was opened and the two huge Mesozoic Age reptiles were brought home to Dinosaur Valley.

A fibreglass Tyrannosaurus rex eyes a Brontosaurus at Dinosaur State Park near Glen Rose.

—Kay White

The Tyrannosaurus rex, made for display at New York's World Fair, was given to the Dinosaur State Park by Sinclair Oil Corporation after its merger with Atlantic Richfield.

Bibliography

Books

Barker, Eugene C. *The Life of Stephen F. Austin.* Austin: University of Texas Press, 1963.

Barker, Eugene C. and Bolton, Herbert Eugene, editors. *With the Makers of Texas.* New York: American Book Co., 1904.

Barker, Eugene C. and Williams, Amelia W., editors. *The Writings of Sam Houston.* Austin: Pemberton Press, 1970.

Barrett, Thomas. *The Great Hanging at Gainesville.* Austin: Texas State Historical Association, 1961.

Battles of Texas. Waco: Texian Press, 1967.

Bolton, Herbert. *Texas in the Middle 18th Century.* Austin: University of Texas Press, 1970.

Brown, John Henry. *History of Texas.* St. Louis: L. E. Daniel, 1893.

Caidin, Martin. *Air Force.* New York: Rinehart, 1957.

Callcott, Wilfred H. *Santa Anna.* Norman: University of Oklahoma Press, 1936.

Castañeda, Carlos E. *Our Catholic Heritage In Texas.* Austin: Von Boeckmann-Jones Co., 1936.

Ceram, C. W. *The First American.* New York: Harcourt Brace Jovanovich, 1971.

Crawford, Ann Fears, editor. *The Eagle, The Autobiography of Santa Anna.* Austin: The Pemberton Press, 1967.

Curry, Jesse. *JFK Assassination File.* Dallas, 1969.

DeShields, James T. *Cynthia Ann Parker.* St. Louis: Chas. B. Woodward Printing and Book Manufacturing Co., 1886.

Dewees, W. B. *Letters from an Early Settler of Texas.* Louisville, Ky.: Morton and Grisnold, 1852.

Eisenhower, Dwight D. *At Ease.* New York: Doubleday and Co., 1967.

Flanagan, Sue. *Sam Houston's Texas.* Austin: University of Texas Press, 1964.

Freund, Max, translator and editor. *Gustav Dresel's Houston Journal.* Austin: University of Texas Press, 1954.

Friedrichs, Irene Hohmann. *History of Goliad.* Goliad: Regal Printers, 1967.

Friend, Llerena B. *Sam Houston, The Great Designer.* Austin: University of Texas Press, 1954.

Gambrell, Herbert. *Mirabeau Buonaparte Lamar, Troubadour and Crusader.* Dallas: Southwest Press, 1934.

Gard, Wayne. *Sam Bass.* Boston: Houghton Mifflin Co., 1936.

Gard, Wayne. *The Chisholm Trail.* Norman: University of Oklahoma Press, 1954.

Glenis, Jr., Carroll V. *The Compact History of the United States Air Force.* New York: Hawthorn Books, Inc., 1936.

Heusinger, Edward W., F. R. G. S. *Early Explorations and Mission Establishments in Texas.* San Antonio: Naylor Co., 1936.

Hodge,Frederick W., ed. *Spanish Explorers in the Southern United States, 1528-1543.* New York: Barnes and Noble, 1959.

Hogan, William Ransom. *The Texas Republic.* Austin: University of Texas Press, 1969.

James, Marquis. *The Raven.* New York: Bobbs Merrill, 1929.

Joutel, Henri. *Joutel's Journal of La Salle's Last Voyage, 1684-7.* Albany, N. Y.: Joseph McDonough Co., 1906.

Johnson, Frank W. *A History of Texas and Texans.* Chicago and New York: American Historical Society, 1914.

Lay, Bennett. *The Lives of Ellis P. Bean.* Austin: University of Texas Press, 1960.

Lea, Tom. *The King Ranch.* Boston: Little Brown and Co., 1957.

Love, Annie C. *History of Navarro County.* Dallas: Southwest Press, 1933.

McComb, David G. *Houston, The Bayou City.* Austin: University of Texas Press, 1969.

Manchester, William. *The Death of a President.* New York: Harper and Row, 1967.

Martin, Paul S.; Quimby, George T.; Collier, Donald. *Indians Before Columbus.* Chicago:

The University of Chicago Press, 1947.

Mooney, Booth. *The Lyndon Johnson Story.* New York: Farrar, Straus, 1964.

Morison, Samuel Eliot. *The Invasion of France and Germany, 1944-1945.* Boston: Little Brown and Co., 1957.

Nance, Joseph M. *Attack and Counter Attack.* Austin: University of Texas Press, 1964..

Newcomb, Jr., W. W. *The Indians of Texas.* Austin: University of Texas Press, 1961.

O'Rourke, Thomas Patrick. *The Franciscan Missions in Texas.* Washington, D. C., 1927.

President's Commission on the Assassination of President Kennedy. *Warren Commission Report.* New York: Associated Press, 1965.

Ramsdell, Charles. *San Antonio, A Historical and Pictorial Guide.* Austin: University of Texas Press, 1959.

Rister, Carl Coke. *Border Captives.* Norman: University of Oklahoma Press, 1940.

Rogers, John William. *The Lusty Texans of Dallas.* New York: E. P. Dutton and Co., 1951.

Sibley, Marilyn. *Travelers in Texas, 1761-1860.* Austin: University of Texas Press, 1967.

Siegel, Stanley. *Big Men Walked Here.* Austin: Jenkins Publishing Co., 1971.

Sleeper, John and Hutchins, J. C. *Waco and McLennan County, Texas, 1876.* Waco: Texian Press, 1966.

Smith, A. Morton. *The First 100 Years in Cooke County.* San Antonio: Naylor Co., 1955.

Smithwick, Noah. *The Evolution of a State.* Austin: Steck Vaughn Co., 1968.

Spence, Hartzell, editorial consultant. *A Great Name in Oil, Sinclair Through Fifty Years.* New York: F. W. Dodge Co./McGraw-Hill, 1966.

Tinkle, Lon. *The Alamo.* New York: Signet Key Books, 1958.

Turner, Martha. *The Life and Times of Jane Long.* Waco: Texian Press, 1969.

Warren, Harris Gaylord. *The Sword Was Their Passport.* Baton Rouge: LSU Press, 1943.

Webb, Walter Prescott, ed. *The Handbook of Texas*. Austin: The Texas State Historical Association, 1952.

White, William S. *The Professional: Lyndon B. Johnson*. Boston: Houghton Mifflin Co., 1964.

Wooten, Dudley G. and Scarff, William G., editors. *A Comprehensive History of Texas*. Dallas, 1898.

Special Publications

Anderson, D. A. "The Masonic Oak of Texas." typescript, 1971.

Atlantic Richfield Company. News Release. Chicago, Illinois, June 3, 1970, July 12, 1970.

The Battle of Velasco. Brazosport: Brazosport Chamber of Commerce.

Blake, R. B. *Nacogdoches*. Nacogdoches: Nacogdoches Historical Society and Chamber of Commerce, 1939.

Duewall, L. A. *The Story of Monument Hill*. La Grange: The La Grange Journal, 1959.

Healer, Samuel B. *A History of Independence Baptist Church 1839-1969 and Related Organizations*. Baptist General Convention of Texas, 1969.

Hoff, Blanche. *San Felipe de Austin*. Sons of the Republic of Texas, 1938.

Tidwell, D. D. *Freemasonry in Brownwood*. Fort Worth: Masonic Home, 1966.

Toepperwein, Fritz A. *O. Henry Almanac*. Boerne, Texas: The Highland Press, Inc.

Magazines

ARCO Spark, XXV, Philadelphia: Atlantic Richfield Co.

Bird, Roland T. "A Dinosaur Walks into the Museum," *Natural History*, XLVII, (February, 1941).

Bird, Roland T. "Thunder in His Footsteps," *Natural History*, XLIII, (May, 1939), 255-302.

Bird, Roland T. "We Captured a 'Live' Brontosaur," *National Geographic,* CV, (May, 1954), 707-722.

Bolton, Herbert E. "The Location of La Salle's Colony on the Gulf of Mexico," *Southwestern Historical Quarterly,* XXVII, (January, 1924), 171-189.

Dabney, Lancaster E. "Louis Aury: First Governor of Texas under the Mexican Republic," *Southwestern Historical Quarterly,* XLII, (October, 1938), 108-116.

Harris, Dilue. "Reminiscences of Mrs. Dilue Harris," *Quarterly of the Texas State Historical Association,* IV, (October, 1900), 160-178.

Kuykendall, J. H. "Reminiscences of Early Texans, A Collection from the Austin Papers," *Quarterly of the Texas State Historical Association,* I, (July, 1903), 35.

Reagan, John. "Expulsion of the Cherokees from East Texas," *Quarterly of the Texas State Historical Association,* I, (July, 1897), 46.

"The Records of an Early Texas Baptist Church," *Quarterly of the Texas State Historical Association,* XII, (July, 1908), 1-60.

Rejebian, Ermane. "La Reunion: The French Colony in Dallas County," *Southwestern Historical Quarterly,* XLIII, (April, 1940).

Smith, Henry. "Reminiscences of Henry Smith," *Texas Historical Association Quarterly,* XIV, (July, 1910), 24-73.

Sparks, S. F. "Recollections of S. F. Sparks," *Quarterly of the Texas State Historical Association,* XII, (July, 1908), 61-79.

The Texan, XIII, Texas City: American Oil Company, (April 17, 1964).

Winfrey, Dorman. "Chief Bowles of the Texas Cherokee," *Texana,* II, (Fall, 1964), 189-202.

Newspapers

Dallas News, November 23, 1963.

Dallas Times Herald, November 22, 1963, April 16, 1972.

Fort Worth Star Telegram, April 17, 18, 19, 20, 21, 27, 28, 1947; November 22, 1963.

Fort Worth Press, November 23, 1963.

Texas City Sun, April 18, 1947, April 12, 1948, April 16, 1972.

Unpublished Writings

Bird, Roland T. Letter to June R. Welch, February 12, 1972.

Callaway, Carolyn. "The 'Runaway Scrape': An Episode of the Texas Revolution," Master's thesis, University of Texas at Austin, June, 1942.

Gazelle, Edward J., public relations division of Atlantic Richfield Co., Chicago, Illinois. Letter to June R. Welch, July 12, 1972.

Hood, Cornelia. "The Life and Career of George Campbell Childress," Master's thesis, University of Texas at Austin, 1938.

Sogorka, Frank R., manager, Dinosaur Exhibit, products division of Atlantic Richfield Co., New York City. Letter to Otice Green, executive assistant to the Governor of Texas, May 8, 1970.

Welch, June R. "The Texas Senatorial Election of 1948," Master's thesis, Texas Tech University, August, 1953.

Wilson, Maurine T. "Philip Nolan and His Activities in Texas," Master's thesis, University of Texas at Austin, June, 1932.

Zander, Mrs. A. H., park attendant at Eisenhower birthplace, Denison. Interview with June R. Welch, January 30, 1972.

Maps

Coursey, Clark; *Courthouses of Texas,* Brownwood, Banner Printing Co., 1962.

INDEX

Abilene, Kansas, 154, 156, 162, 164, 180
Adaesanos, 50, 52
Adams, Ernest, 2
Adams-Oñis Treaty, 62
advertising, 182
Aguayo, Marquis de San Miguel de, 38, 44, 48
Aguirre, Pedro de, 24
airplane, 168
Alabama, 70, 128, 146
Alamo, 28, 86, 88, 96, 98, 100, 102, 106
Alamo Plaza, 160
Alarcón, Martín de, 24, 28
Alarcón expedition, 24
alcalde, 36, 72, 86
Alexandria, Virginia, 168
Alhaja, Martín, 12
Allen, Augustus, 116
Allen, John, 116
Allies, 170
Alsbury, Mrs. Horace, 86
Alta Mira, 82
Alto, 8
Alvarez, Francisca, 90
American Museum of Natural History, 2, 4, 182
ammonium nitrate, 172
Anahuac, 76, 98
Anderson, 82
Anderson County, 78, 82, 110
Anderson, Kenneth, 82
annexation, 138
Apache, 30, 42, 44
Appomattox, 152
aqueduct, 46
Aranama, 48
Arizona, 102, 180
Arkansas, 66
Arredondo, Joaquín de, 62
assassination, 176
Atascosito, 72
Atlantic fleet, 170
Atlantic Richfield Oil Company, 182
Attoyac River, 52
Augusta, Georgia, 150
Aury, Louis-Michel, 56, 60
Austin, 4, 38, 64, 72, 104, 116, 126, 132, 136, 146, 166, 180
Austin colonies, 10, 66, 68, 82, 84, 98, 108
Austin County, 68, 72
Austin, John, 76, 114
Austin, Moses, 66, 68
Austin, Stephen F., 66, 68, 76, 114, 122, 128
Au Texas, 140
Baines, George Washington, 134
Baker, William, 146
Barataria Bay, 58
Barkley, Alben, 178
Barnard, Joseph, 94
Barnes, Seaborn, 158
Barron, T. H., 122
Barry, Buck, 124
Barton, 124
Bass, Sam, 158
Bastrop, Baron de, 66
Barrington, 138
Battle Creek, 124
Battleship Texas Commission, 170
Baylor University, 2, 4, 134, 140
Bayonne, France, 58
Bean, Ellis, 54
Beason's Ford, 98

Beckley Street, 176
Beeman, James, 136
Belfast, 54
Belgium, 140
Belgrade, 44
Belknap, William, 160
Bexar County, 24, 28, 30, 36, 38, 42, 44, 46, 66, 86, 150, 160, 168
Bill's Creek, 44
Bird, Roland, 2, 4, 182
Bird's Fort, 136
black beans, 142
Blanco County, 178
Blondel, M., 30
Bolivar Point, 62, 64
Bolivia, 66
Bollinger Creek, 72
Bolton, Herbert Eugene, 16
Bonham, 136
Bonham, James, 86, 88
Borden Company, 72
Borden, Gail, 116
Borden, Thomas, 116
Bowie, James, 86, 100
Bradburn, John Davis, 76
Bouchu, Francis, 42
Bowles, Chief, 130
Boyd, 122
Brazoria, 64, 76, 114, 138
Brazoria County, 76, 108, 114
Brazos Guards, 88
Brazos River, 50, 70, 72, 76, 98, 104, 122
Brigham, Asa, 114
British, 48, 58
brontosaur, 2, 4, 182
Brooklyn College, 4
Brown, Barnum, 4, 182
Brownwood, 104
Bryan, John Neely, 136
Bucareli, 50
Buchanan, James, 178
Buckner, 10
Buffalo Bayou, 100, 102, 116
Bullock, Richard, 132
Burleson, Rufus, 130, 134
Burnet, David, 70, 102, 108
Burnham's crossing, 98
Butler, Benjamin, 150
Byars, Noah, 104, 106
Cabeza de Vaca, Alvar Núñez, 10, 12, 14
Cabeza de Vaca, Martín, 12
Cabeza de Vaca, Teresa, 12
cabildo, 36
Cadiz, Spain, 12
Caddo, 22, 26, 52, 124
Cadillac, De la Mothe, 38
Caldwell, J. P., 114
Caldwell, Mathew, 142
California, 102, 118, 136, 178
California Street, 152
Cameron, 84
Cameron, Ewen, 142
Camino Real, 52, 66
Campeche, 60
Canada, 16
Canary Islanders, 36
cannibalism, 10
capital, 50, 126
carnosaur, 4
Carranza, Andrés Dorantes de, 12
Carswell Air Force Base, 174
Casa Blanca, 170

Cherbourg, 170
Cherokee, 116, 122, 128, 130, 144, 154
Cherokee County, 8
Chesapeake Bay, 170
Chicago, 156
chicken defense, 30
Chihuahua, 54
Childress, George, 106
Chinook, 8
Chisholm, Jesse, 154
Chisholm Trail, 156, 158
Choctaw, 128
Christian Church, 78
Cibola, 14
Civil War, 124, 154, 160
Claiborne, Governor, 58
Clark, Edward, 146
Clark, Horace, 134
Coahuila, 24, 72
Coahuiltecan Indians, 38
Coahuiltecan language, 42
coastal plain, 10
Coca Cola, 176
Coco, 48
Coffee, Holland, 136
Cole's settlement, 134
Collins, Joel, 158
Collinsworth, James, 126
colonists, 36, 72, 76, 140
Colorado County, 96, 98, 118
Colorado River, 38, 72, 98, 102
Columbia, 56, 100, 108, 116
Columbia University, 164
Columbus, 96, 98, 118
Comanche, 42, 50, 110, 112
Commercio Plaza, 72
Committee of Public Saftey, 150
Compostela, 14
Concepción, 38, 42, 88
Concepción, battle of, 100
Confederacy, 124, 136, 146, 152, 170
Connally, John, 174
Connally, Mrs. John, 174
Conner, Henry, 128
Conrad, Edward, 106
Considerant, Victor, 140
Consultation of 1835, 72, 78, 104, 118, 128
Cooke County, 152
Copano, 88
Coronado, Francisco Vásquez de, 14
Cordova, Vincente, 126
Corpus Christi, 10, 24
Corsicana, 124
Cós, Martín Perfecto de, 86, 88, 102
Cotten, G. B., 72, 118
cotton, 70
Cotton Plant, The, 118
cottonwood, 28
Cotulla, 178
Council of the Indies, 36
Creek Indians, 8, 136
Cujame, 48
Culpepper County, Virginia, 62
Customhouses, 76
D Day, 170
Dallas, 136, 140, 156, 158, 174
Dallas County, 136, 174, 176
Davis, John, 78
Dawson, Nicholas Mosby, 142
Deadwood, 158
Decatur, 156

191

declarations of independence, 84, 106, 134
Delaware Indians, 110, 112, 128
De León, Alonso, 16, 22
Democratic Party, 174
Denison, 162, 164
Denton County, 158
Denton Mare, 158
Department of Public Safety, 172
Dewees, W. B., 98
Dickenson, Mrs. Almeron, 86, 100
Dickenson, Angelina, 100
Dickinson County, Kansas, 162, 164
Dickson, Jim, 152
Dies, Martin, 178
dinosaurs, 2, 182
Dinosaur State Park, 182
District of Columbia, 144
Dodge City, 156
Don Quixote, 58
Douglas, 38
Dresel, Gustav, 116
Duhaut, 18
Dumas, J. P., 136
Duran, Guadalupe Ruiz, 100
Durham, Connecticutt, 66
Dusenberry, John E., 142
Duty, 110
Eagle Lake, 96
Eagle Pass, 168
Eastland, William Mosby, 142
East Texas, 22, 28, 44, 50, 52, 128
East Texas Indians, 8, 24
East Texas missions, 24, 26, 42, 46, 48
Ecuador, 56
Ehrenberg, Herman, 90
Eisenhower, David, 164
Eisenhower, Dwight, 162, 164, 174
Eisenhower, Earl, 162
Eisenhower, Ida, 162
Eisenhower Library, 180
El Alamo, 28
Elkhart, 78
Ellsworth, 156
Elm Street, 174, 176
embezzlement, 166
empresarios, 68, 84
England, 82
English, 48, 58
English Channel, 170
Erath, George B., 122
Espada, 42, 46
Espada Ditch Company, 46
Espinosa, Father Isidro Felix de, 24
Espíritu Santo de Zúniga, Nuestra Señora
    del, 36, 48, 94
Estevanico, 12
explosion, 172
Fannin, 94
Fannin County, 136
Fannin, James Walker, 86, 88, 100, 114
Fanthorp, Henry, 82
Fanthorp Inn, 82
Fayette County, 142
Fields, Richard, 128
filibustering, 58, 62
Filisola, Vicente, 102, 108
Fisher, William S., 142
Flores, Gil, 50
Florida, 12, 14
Fort Bend County, 100
Fort Defiance, 88
Fort Gibson, 112
Fort Inglish, 136
Fort Myer, Virginia, 168
Fort Parker, 110, 124

Fort St. Louis, 16, 18, 22
Fort Sam Houston, 128
Fort Worth, 156, 174
forts, 76
Foulois, Benjamin, 168
Fourier, Francois, 140
France, 16, 30, 48, 50, 132, 140
Franciscans, 24, 26, 30, 36, 42, 44, 46, 52
Frankfort, Kentucky, 54
Franklin, 124
Fredonian rebellion, 128
French, 16, 22, 24, 26, 36, 44, 50, 58, 132,
    172
French and Indian War, 48
Frio, 42
Frost, Robert, 110
Frost, Samuel, 110
Gaines, James, 106
Gainesville, 152
Galveston, 10, 12, 56, 60, 62, 106, 132, 146,
    172
Galveston Bay, 56
Galveston County, 10, 12, 56, 58, 172
Gambrell, Herbert, 126
Garcia, Bartolme, 42
Garcitas Creek, 16
Garner, John Nance, 174
Garrison, George, 68
Georgia, 70, 88, 104, 118, 126, 146, 150
Germany, 116, 170
Gibraltar, 170
Gilbert, Mabel, 136
Glen Rose, 2, 182
gold seekers, 136
Goldwater, Barry, 180
Goliad, 48, 68, 88, 94, 114
Goliad County, 48, 88, 90
Goliad Massacre, 90, 94
Gonzales, 86, 88, 96, 98, 102, 104, 142
Gonzales, José, 50
Grandcamp, 170, 172
Great Serpent Mound, 8
Greyhound bus station, 176
Grimes County, 18, 70, 82
Groce, Jared, 70
Groce's Ferry, 70
Grand Lodge, 114
Grant, Ulysses S., 160
Graves, Henry, 134
Gray, F. C., 118
Gray, William, 106
Grayson County, 162
Grayson, Peter, 126
Great Barrington, Massachusetts, 138
Grimes, A. W., 158
Guadalupe mission, 48, 50, 52
Guerrero, 142
Gulf of Mexico, 12, 16, 60, 178
Haciendo Salado, 142
Hall, John, 104
Hamilton, Robert, 106
hangings, 152
Hardeman, Bailey, 106
Harper's Magazine, 160
Harris County, 102, 116, 170
Harris, Dilue, 96
Harris, Ira, 96
Harrisburg, 72, 100
Harvard University, 180
Hasinai, 26, 38, 50, 52
Hawkins, Joseph, 68
head flattening, 8
Hemphill, John, 138
Henderson, 124
Henderson County, 128

Henderson, J. Pinckney, 138
Henderson, W. F., 124
Hendryx, 80
Herff, Ferdinand, 160
Herrera, Jose Manuel de, 56
Hidalgo, Francisco, 38
hidalgos, 36
Hiens, 18
High Flyer, 172
Hill County, 54, 154
Hiroshima, 172
Hispañola, 58
Holland, 124
Holland, J. H., 114
Holland Lodge, 114
Honduras, 166
Hoover Library, 180
Hord's Ridge, 136
Hotel Texas, 174
Houston, 72, 82, 88, 96, 98, 102, 108, 114,
    116, 132, 140, 172, 174, 178
Houston, Andrew Jackson, 178
Houston County, 66
Houston, Margaret Lea, 134
Houston, Sam, 84, 86, 96, 100, 114, 116, 126,
    128, 130, 134, 138, 142, 144, 150, 178
Houston, Sam Jr., 146
Houston Post, 166
Humphreys, Frederic, 168
Huntsville, 146
Hyde Park, 180
Illinois, 174
independence, 86, 102, 104
Independence, Missouri, 180
Independence, Texas, 134, 138
Independence Baptist Church, 134
Independence Convention, 106
Independence Female Academy, 134
Indians, 8, 12, 14, 28, 36, 42, 44, 46, 62, 116,
    124, 126, 128, 158
Indian Territory, 112, 130, 154, 156
inn, 82
Ioni Indians, 124
Ireland, 124
irrigation ditches, 28
Iwo Jima, 170
Jack, Patrick, 76
Jackson, Andrew, 58, 108, 144
Jackson, Frank, 158
Jackson, Jeanie, 162
Japanese, 170
Jefferson, Thomas, 54
Jefferson Street, 176
Jenny, 158
Johnson City High School, 178
Johnson, Frank, 86
Johnson, Lyndon, 134, 178, 180
Jonas, Louis, 182
Jones, Anson, 114, 126, 130, 132, 138
Joutel, Henri, 16, 18
Kansas, 102, 154, 156, 162
Kansas City, 154, 156
Karankawa, 10, 48, 70
Karnack, 178
Karnes, Henry, 100
Katy, 162
Keeran, Claude, 16
Kellogg, 110
Kennard, Rachael, 82
Kennedy, John, 174, 178, 180
Kennedy Library, 180
Kentucky, 62, 76
Key, Francis Scott, 144
Kiamatia, 64
Kian, 64

Kickapoo, 124, 128
King, Richard, 160
King's Highway, 66
Kingsville, 160
Kiowa, 110
Kleberg, Richard, 178
Kounty Creek, 134
La Bahía, 64, 88, 104
La Bahía Road, 104
Lafitte, Jean, 56, 58, 60, 62
Lafitte, Pierre, 58, 60
La Grange, 142
Lahm, Frank, 168
Lamar, M. B., 64, 106, 116, 122, 126, 130, 138
Lamartine, 122
Lane, Walter, 124, 142
Lanier, Sidney, 160
Laredo, 142, 168
La Salle, Rène Robert Cavelier, Sieur de, 10, 16, 18, 22, 48, 166
Law of April 6, 1830, 84
Lea, Nancy, 134
lead mining, 66
Lee, Robert E., 160
Leftwich, Robert, 84
Lewis and Clark, 8
Liberty, 76
Limestone County, 110
Lincoln, Abraham, 146
Liotot, 18
Lipan, 42
Little Rock, 66, 68
Little Rocky Creek, 134
Lively, The, 76, 108
Long, James, 60, 62, 64
Long, Jane, 62, 64
Long, Mary James, 64
longhorns, 154, 156
Los Adaes, 50
Los Ais, 50
Louis XIV, 16
Louis Phillipe, 132
Louisiana, 16, 26, 30, 50, 52, 54, 58, 66, 96, 114, 146
Louisiana Purchase, 62, 68
Love Field, 174
Lubbock, Francis, 116
Lyndon Baines Johnson Library, 180
Madelina, 70
Madison, James, 58
Main Plaza, 150
Maldonado, Alonzo del Castillo, 12
Malhado Isle, 10, 12, 14
Mann, Gerald C., 178
Mansfield, Battle of, 124
Margil de Jesús, Antonio, 26, 30
Market Hall, 174
Marsalis Park, 136
Martínez, Antonio María, 64, 66
Masonic Lodge, 114
Masonic Oak, 114
Massanet, Damian, 16, 18, 22, 24
Matagorda, 56, 60
Matagorda Bay, 16, 36, 48
Matamoras, 88
McCoy, Joseph, 154, 156
McCulloch, Ben, 150
McDonald, M. N., 180
McFarland, Ernest, 180
McFarland, John, 72
McLennan County, 122
McLennan, John, 122
McLennan, Laughlin, 122

McLennan, Neil, 122
Mead, 78
Medina, 42
Menger Hotel, 166
Menger, William, 160
Mercer, Peter M., 104
Mexican troops, 100, 106, 108
Mexican War, 68, 124, 150
Mexicans, 28, 76, 88, 142
Mexico, 10, 12, 22, 36, 56, 60, 64, 68, 72, 76, 90, 94, 102, 108, 126, 138
Mexico City, 14, 24, 50, 64, 128, 142
Mier expedition, 142
Milam County, 84
Milam Lodge, 114
Military Plaza, 72
Mina, Francisco Xavier, 56, 60, 76
missions, 22, 28, 30, 36, 42, 44, 48
Mississippi, 18, 54, 58, 100, 146
Mississippi River, 16
Missouri, 66, 154
Missouri Botanical Gardens, 140
Missouri, Kansas and Texas Railway Company, 164
Mujeres Island, 60
mob, 152
Monclova, 66
Monsanto Chemical Company, 172
Montgomery County, 112
Montopolis, 126
Montreal, 16
Monument Hill, 142
Moore, Maurice, 158
Moranger, 18
Morfí, Juan, 30
Morocco, 170
motor oil, 182
mound builders, 8
Mound Prairie, 8
Mound Street, 8
Murphy, Jim, 158
mustanging, 54
mutiny, 56
Nacogdoche Indians, 26, 52
Nacogdoches, 8, 26, 50, 52, 54, 62, 68, 76, 82, 110, 114
Nacogdoches County, 26, 38, 44, 50, 52
Nadaco, 44
Nagasaki, 172
Napoleonic Wars, 58
Narváez, Pánfilo de, 12
Nashville, 84
Nashville-on-the-Brazos, 84
Natchez, Mississippi, 54, 62
Natchitoches, 50, 52, 66
National Youth Administration, 178
NATO, 164
Nava, Pedro de, 54
naval architecture, 170
Navarre, King of, 12
Navarro County, 124
Navasota, 18
Nebraska, 158
Neches, battle of the, 128
Neches River, 128
Negro Indian fighters, 70
Neri, Felipe, 66
Nevada, 102
Nevantin, 26
New Deal, 178
New Granada, 56
New Mexico, 102, 158
New Orleans, 54, 56, 58, 60, 62, 68, 132, 140, 150
New Orleans, battle of, 84

New Philippines, 52
New Spain, 28, 62
New York, 4, 100, 116, 118, 166, 180
New York World's Fair, 182
Nixon, L. D., 110
Nixon, Richard, 174, 180
Nocona, Peta, 112
Nolan, Philip, 54
Norfolk Navy Yard, 170
North Carolina, 166
Northern Standard, 112
North Texas, 152
Normandy, 170
Nueces River, 42
Nuestra Señora de Guadalupe de los Nacogdoches, 26, 52
Nuestro Señora del Pilar de Nacgodoches, 50
Nuestra Señora del Refugio, 10
Nuestra Señora de la Purísima Concepción, 38
Nuestra Señora de Loreto, 48, 88
Nuestra Señora de los Dolores, 42
Oconor, Hugo, 50
O'Daniel, W. Lee, 178
Odin, John, 132
Ohio, 144
Ohio River, 16
Oklahoma, 102
Oklahoma City, 154
Old San Antonio Road, 66
Old Providence Island, 56
Olivares, Antonio de San Buenaventura, 24, 28, 30
Omaha Beach, 170
Oswald, Lee Harvey, 176
Oxford University, 2
Pacific, 68, 126, 170
Paluxy River, 2, 4
Panama, 56
Paraguay, 14
Paris, 56, 174
Parker, Benjamin, 80, 110
Parker, Cynthia Ann, 110, 112, 124
Parker, Daniel, 78, 110
Parker, Granny, 110
Parker, James, 110, 112
Parker, John, 110, 112
Parker, Quanah, 112
Parker, Silas, 110
Parkland Hospital, 174
Patron, Augustin, 48
Payaya, 24
Peace Party, 152
Pearl Harbor, 170, 178
Pensacola, 30
Pérez, Ignacio, 62, 64
Peru, 22
Peters Colony, 136, 152
Phelps, James, 114
physicians, 12
Piedras, José de las, 76
pigs, 132
Pilgrim Church, 78, 110
Pilgrim, Thomas, 72
pirates, 56, 58
Placedo, 16
Plummer, James, 110, 112
Plummer, Rachel, 110, 112
Polk, James K., 138, 144
Pond Creek, 122
port, 172
Porter, Jack, 178
Porter, William Sydney, 160, 166
Potosi, 66

Poverty Point mounds, 8
presidios, 16, 48, 90
Preston, 156
Primitive Baptist Church, 78
privateers, 56, 58, 60
provisional government, 62
pueblo, 30, 38
Querétarian, 26
Quarley, 78
Ramón, José Domingo, 26, 44, 48
Ramón expedition, 24, 38
Rancho de Lucana, 52
Rancho Santa Gertrudis, 160
rangers, 122
Rayburn, Sam, 178
Reagan, John, 128
Redland Lodge, 114
Red River, 62, 128, 136, 156
Red River Station, 156
Republic of Texas, 82, 84, 100, 102, 114, 116,
  118, 122, 126, 128, 132, 134, 138, 144
Reverchon, Julien, 140
Richmond, 62, 64, 66, 100, 170
Rio Grande, 24, 28, 38, 48, 66, 68, 96, 108,
  142
Rio de la Plata, 14
Ripley, E. W., 62
Ripperdá, Baron de, 50
Robeline, Louisiana, 50
Roberts, Oran, 120, 146
Robertson, Felix, 84
Robertson, Sterling, 84
Robertson's Colony, 84
Robinson, Andrew, 104
Robinson, James W., 104
Roman Catholic Church, 78
Rogers, John William, 136
Rolling Stone, 166
Roosevelt, Franklin, 174, 178
Roosevelt Library, 180
Roosevelt, Theodore, 160, 166
Rose, Pleasant, 96
Ross County, Ohio, 8
Ross, L.S., 112
Rouen, France, 16
Round Rock, 158
Rubí, Marquis de, 26, 50
Ruby, Jack, 176
Ruiz, Francisco, 86
Runaway Scrape, 70, 72, 96, 98
Rusk, T. J., 94, 102, 128, 138
Russell, Alexander, 114
Russia, 166
Ryals, Jim, 2, 4
Sabine River, 52, 62, 66, 96, 106
Saget, 18
Saligny, Alphonse de, 132
Saltillo, 44, 72, 84
Sancho Panza, 58
Santo Domingo, 56
Saint Anthony, 24
St. Denis, Louis de, 26, 38
Saint John, 44
St. Joseph, 154
St. Louis, 96, 140, 154
Salado, battle of the, 142
San Antonio, 22, 24, 26, 28, 30, 36, 42, 44,
  48, 50, 52, 54, 66, 68, 86, 88, 96, 100, 132,
  142, 160, 166, 174
San Antonio Catholic Archdiocese, 38
San Antonio Conservation Society, 46
San Antonio de Valero, 24, 28, 30, 86
San Antonio River, 24, 28, 30, 36, 38
San Augustine, 82, 114

San Felipe de Austin, 68, 72, 82, 98, 104,
  114, 118
San Fernando Cathedral, 36
San Francisco de la Espada, 22, 42, 46
San Francisco de los Neches, 22
San Francisco de los Tejas, 22, 24, 26, 38,
  66
San Jacinto, 72, 98, 100, 108, 116, 118, 122,
  124, 126, 138, 142, 170
San José, 30, 42, 44
San José de los Nazonis, 42, 44
San José y San Miguel de Aguayo, 24, 30,
  44
San Juan Bautista, 38, 44
San Juan Capistrano, 42, 44
San Marcos, 178
San Miguel de Linares, 30
San Patricio, 88
San Pedro Springs, 24, 28
Sánchez, Benito, 44
Santa Anna, 72, 86, 88, 90, 96, 98, 100, 102,
  106, 108, 114, 118, 126, 128, 142
Sarahville de Viesca, 84
sauropod, 2
Schoolbook Depository, 174, 176
Scotland, 122
Scott, Winfield, 150
Secession, 146, 150, 152
Secretary of State, 132
Secularization, 28, 30, 38, 42
Sedalia, 154
Selfridge, Thomas, 168
Sesma, Joaquin, 98
Seville, 14
Shawnee, 128
Shawnee Trail, 154, 156
Sheppard, Morris, 178
Sheridan, Philip, 160
Sherman, Sidney, 100
Shuler, Ellis, 2
Signal Corps, 168
Sinclair Dinosaur Book, 182
Sinclair Oil Company, 4, 182
Slaves, 70, 78
Smith, Ashbel, 106
Smith, Erastus "Deaf", 100
Smith, Henry, 86, 104
Smith, Robert, 130
Smithsonian Institution, 4
Smithwick, Noah, 72, 118, 120
smuggling, 58, 60
Solís, Gasper José de, 10
Somervell, Alexander, 142
Somervell County, 2, 182
South America, 56
South Carolinia, 104
South Texas, 156
Southern Methodist University, 4
Southwest Texas State Teachers College,
  178
Spain, 14, 16, 22, 26, 30, 48, 50, 56, 68, 160
Spaniards, 10, 12, 14, 22, 26, 52, 54, 56, 58,
  62, 66, 72, 76
Spanish-American War, 170
Spanish cattle, 154
Spanish law, 38, 54
Sparks, S. F., 102
Speaker, 178
Spraggins, Thomas, 134
Springfield, 82
Springfield, Illinois, 154
Stafford's Point, 96
Stanberry, William, 144
Steamboat House, 146
Stephen F. Austin State University, 52

Stevenson, Coke, 178
Stone Fort, 52, 54
surgery, 12
Switzerland, 140
synthetic rubber, 172
Tamique, 48
Tampa Bay, 14
Taylor, Claudia, 178
Taylor, Zachary, 112, 150
Tehuacana, 124
Tejas Indians, 38
temple mounds, 8
Tennessee, 62, 84, 106, 136, 138, 144, 154
Tenth Street, 176
Terán, Domingo de los Rios, 24, 66
Texarkana, 8
Texas, 28, 104, 170
Texas Army, 70, 94, 108, 126, 144
Texas City, 172
Texas Congress, 78, 120, 136, 138
Texas Cretaceous, 2
Texas fever, 154
The Texas Gazette, 72
Texas Revolution, 68
The Texas Telegraph and Texas Register,
  72
Texas theater, 176
Tippit, J. D., 176
Tonkawa, 10
Tonti, Henri de, 18
trailing, 154
Travis County, 126, 132, 158, 166, 178
Travis, William Barret, 64, 76, 86, 88, 96, 100
Triceratops, 182
Trinity River, 50, 136, 140
Troup, George, 126
Truman Library, 180
Tucker, Charley, 158
Turtle Bayou Resolutions, 76
Twenty-One Club, 162
Twiggs, David E., 150
treaties of Velasco, 108
Tyler, John, 138
Tyler, 162
Tyrannosaurus, 182
Ugartechea, Domingo de, 76, 118
Union Pacific, 154
Unionists, 146, 152
United States, 62, 126, 138
United States Army, 54, 168
United States Department of the Interior, 46
U.S.S. Maine, 170
U.S.S. Texas, 170
University of Texas at Austin, 4, 180
Upper Louisiana, 66
Urrea, José, 88, 90, 94, 114
Utah, 102
Uvalde, 174
Valero, Marquis de, 28
Van Buren, Arkansas, 136
Van Zandt County, 128
Velasco, 76, 88, 100
Velasco Island, 12
Venezuela, 56
Vera Cruz, 108
Vera, Francisco de, 12
Vergara, Father, 44
viceroy, 24, 28, 44, 48, 50, 52
Victoria, 48, 88, 90
Victoria County, 16
Vienna, Austria, 122
Vietnam, 180
Villa de Bexar, 28
Villa San Fernando, 24, 36
Village Creek, battle of, 136

Vince's Bridge, 100, 102
Violet, 124
Virginia, 66, 70, 144
Waco, 122, 124, 156
Waco Indians, 122
Walker County, 144, 146
Waller County, 70
Waller, Edwin, 76
Warren, Harris, 58
Washington, 68, 70, 86, 100, 104, 106, 120,
    132, 134, 138, 144, 150, 178
Washington County, 104, 134, 138
Weches, 22
West Branch, Iowa, 180
West Point, 88, 162, 164
Wharton, 120
Wharton, Clarence, 94
Wharton, John, 114
White Rock Creek, 136
Wichita, 122
Wichita, Kansas, 154
Wilkinson, James, 54, 62
Wilkinson, Jane, 62
Williams, Samuel, 84
Williamson County, 120, 158
Williamson, Annexus, 120
Williamson, Robert, 118, 120
Wilson, Woodrow, 170
Woll, Adrian, 142
Works Progress Administration, 4
World War II, 162, 164
Wright, Orville, 168
Wright, Wilbur, 168
Wyoming, 102
Yale University, 182
Yanaguana, 24
Ybarbo, Antonio Gil, 26, 50, 52
Young County, 152
Yucatan, 60
Zilker Park, 38

June Rayfield Welch was born in Brownwood, Texas, November 24, 1927, and holds degrees from Texas Christian University, the University of Texas at Arlington, Texas Tech University, and George Washington University. He is an attorney and has been Academic Dean at the University of Dallas, where he is presently Chairman of the Department of History. His published books include A FAMILY HISTORY, THE TEXAS COURTHOUSE, and TEXAS; NEW PERSPECTIVES, which has been adopted for high school use by more than 500 Texas school districts.